WITHDRAWN

D0860065

Presented to:

_____

Presented by:

_____

Date:

_____

Glory to God, this wondrous morn,

On earth the Savior Christ is born.

Bliss Carman

Wake Technical Community College
9101 Fayetteville Road
Raleigh, NC 27603-5696

THE BIG BOOK OF

CHRISTMAS JOY

An Inspirational Treasury to Celebrate the Season

HOWARD BOOKS
A Division of Simon & Schuster
New York   London   Toronto   Sydney

Our purpose at Howard Books is to:
· *Increase faith* in the hearts of growing Christians
· *Inspire holiness* in the lives of believers
· *Instill hope* in the hearts of struggling people everywhere
Because He's coming again!

Published by Howard Books, a division of Simon & Schuster, Inc.
1230 Avenue of the Americas, New York, NY 10020
www.howardpublishing.com

The Big Book of Christmas Joy © 2008 by Dave Bordon and Associates, LLC

All rights reserved, including the right to reproduce this book or portions thereof in any form whatsoever. For information, address Howard Subsidiary Rights Department, 1230 Avenue of the Americas, New York, NY 10020.

ISBN-13: 978-1-4165-7107-0
ISBN-10:   1-4165-7107-8

10 9 8 7 6 5 4 3 2 1

HOWARD and colophon are registered trademarks of Simon & Schuster, Inc.

Manufactured in the United States of America

For information regarding special discounts for bulk purchases, please contact: Simon & Schuster Special Sales at 1-800-456-6798 or business@simonandschuster.com.

Project developed by Bordon Books, Tulsa, Oklahoma
Project writing and compilation by Snapdragon Group℠ Editorial Services
Edited by Chrys Howard
Cover and interior design by Jennith Moncrief, Bordon Books
Cover photograph by Inmagine

For Scripture quotation permissions, see page 313, which constitutes an extension of this copyright page.

PN
6071
.C6
B5
2008

yoC
0 = 227199870

CONTENTS

Christmas Is
LOVE

Dear friends, let us love one another,

for love comes from God.

1 JOHN 4:7 NIV

CHRISTMAS IS LOVE

There would be no Christmas were it not for love—God's love. His was a love so great that it formed a bridge from the hearts of men to the throne of Heaven. It was a love so great that it transformed sinful, disgraced men and women into brightly shining children of the Most High God. That love came to us in the form of a human baby graced with a divine lineage. His name is Jesus, and He is God's only begotten Son.

It is said that a gift is not truly a gift unless it costs the giver in some sacrificial way. In that sense, God gave the only gift possible. He had no other Son, only Jesus. What must He have felt for us—willful creation that we were—that He was compelled to bless us so richly? Only great, unspeakable, inexplicable, undeserved, perfect love—God's love—could be so sweet. That love is what Christmas is all about.

Loving Father, help us remember the birth of Jesus, that we may share in the song of the angels, the gladness of the shepherds, and the worship of the wise men.

Close the door of hate and open the door of love all over the world.

Let kindness come with every gift and good desires with every greeting.

Deliver us from evil by the blessing which Christ brings, and teach us to be merry with clear hearts.

May the Christmas morning make us happy to be Thy children, and the Christmas evening bring us to our beds with grateful thoughts, forgiving and forgiven, for Jesus' sake.

Amen.

Robert Louis Stevenson

THE CHRISTMAS PARADOX

Author Unknown

It is *in loving*—not in being loved—
the heart is blest;
It is *in giving*—not in seeking gifts—
we find our quests. . . .

Whatever be thy longing and thy need,
That do thou give;
So shall thy soul be fed, and thou indeed,
Shalt truly live.

Thanks be to God for His *unspeakable Gift—*

indescribable

inestimable

incomparable

inexpressible

precious beyond words.

Lois LeBar

A CHRISTMAS KIND OF LOVE

Janet Lynn Mitchell

I stood in awe as I watched her faith being lived out. What had brought her to this moment had faded, and now she concentrated on the task before her. As her contractions progressed, I gently dried her forehead from the sweat of labor. I held her hand, and she grasped mine with determination. One moment we laughed, and the next I joined her and tears flowed freely. We both knew it. Today our lives would change—forever.

Hours passed, and her contractions intensified. "You're doing great!" I assured her when the pain reached her threshold. Soon, the doctor arrived, and we were whisked to the delivery room. I took a seat by her side and continued to coach her. The room was cold, yet warmed by the miracle about to take place. My heart pounded as I listened to the piercing sound of her labor cries. I brushed her hair away from her face and admired the inner strength of this young woman.

One final push and the baby was born. We held hands as the doctor cut the cord separating mother and child. The room was silent except for the sounds of a newborn's cry. My heart raced as I watched the nurse carefully bundle the baby. In seconds, she placed the precious infant in my arms—*in my arms.* For the young woman who had just given birth had chosen me to become the mother of her child.

The baby was beautiful. I was so moved that I couldn't speak. While I cradled my daughter for the first time, I glanced at her birth mother. Her eyes spoke volumes. She smiled through her tears while she watched me begin to bond with my priceless gift. I saw the fight within her. With a quiver, I nodded to assure her of my promised vows to motherhood. She then reached over and ran her finger along the baby's cheek. "She is beautiful," were her words. Soon, the nurse said it was time to go. I stood and brought the baby to the lips of her birth mother. I watched as she tenderly and with great love kissed her precious infant good-bye. My voice trembled as I tried to find appropriate words to express my thanks. Before this day I had never comprehended such an act of love, such faith in action and courage despite fear.

Walking to the newborn nursery, I was amazed at the vision that God the Father played in slow motion across my mind. I saw Him touching His Holy Child and cradling Him within His bosom. I pondered and wondered if God, too, kissed Baby Jesus good-bye just before He handed Him to Mary. Of course—now I understood. The pieces had come together. The plan, the provision God had created for my redemption, had been born. Adequate words of thanks failed me. God, too, had given up His Child, and for me. I cried as my heart swelled with praise. At last I understood a Christmas kind of love, a love that gives beyond comprehension and a love that gives in spite of pain.[1]

CHRISTMAS FUDGE

This is a gift of Christmas love you can share.

Ingredients:

1 bag (18 ounces) semisweet chocolate chips

1 can (14 ounces) sweetened condensed milk

Dash of salt

½ chopped nuts, optional

2 tsp. vanilla extract

Instructions:

Place the chocolate chips, sweetened condensed milk, and salt in a saucepan or double-boiler. Stir over low heat until the chips are melted. Remove from heat and add nuts and vanilla. Line an 8-inch square pan with waxed paper and spread the mixture evenly. Chill until firm. Cut into squares. Wrap in red or green plastic wrap, add a bow, and share with neighbors, friends, family—anyone you would like to touch with the light of God's love.

A CHRISTMAS LIST

Swedish Proverb

Fear less, *hope more;*

Eat less, *chew more;*

Whine less, *breathe more;*

Talk less, *say more;*

Hate less, *love more;*

And all good things will be yours.

Here is love,

that God sent his Son, . . .

his Son who never offended,

his Son who was

always his delight.

John Bunyan

O HOLY NIGHT

Placide Cappeau
Translated by John S. Dwight

Led by the light of faith serenely beaming,
With glowing hearts by His cradle we stand.
So led by light of a star sweetly gleaming,
Here came the wise men from Orient land.
The King of kings lay thus in lowly manger,
In all our trials born to be our Friend! . . .

Truly He taught us to love
one another;
His law is love and His
Gospel is peace.
Chains shall He break
for the slave is our brother
And in His name all
oppression shall cease.
Sweet hymns of joy in grateful
chorus raise we,
Let all within us praise His
holy Name!

Blessed is the season

that engages the whole world

in a *conspiracy of love!*

Hamilton Wright Mabie

Selfishness makes
Christmas a burden;
Love makes it
a delight.

Author Unknown

LOVE, FIRST CORINTHIANS 13–STYLE

Adapted from 1 Corinthians 13

Sharon Jaynes

If I decorate my house perfectly with lovely plaid bows, strands of twinkling lights, and shiny glass balls, but do not show love to my family—*I'm just another decorator.*

If I slave away in the kitchen, baking dozens of Christmas cookies, preparing gourmet meals, and arranging a beautifully adorned table at mealtime, but do not show love to my family—*I'm just another cook.*

If I work at the soup kitchen, carol in the nursing home, and give all that I have to charity, but do not show love to my family—*it profits me nothing.*

If I trim the spruce with shimmering angels and crocheted snowflakes, attend a myriad of holiday parties, and sing in the choir's cantata but do not focus on Christ, *I have missed the point.*

Love stops the cooking to hug the child.

Love sets aside the decorating to kiss the husband.

Love is kind, though harried and tired.

Love doesn't envy another home that has coordinated Christmas china and table linens.

Love doesn't yell at the kids to get out of your way.

Love doesn't give only to those who are able to give in return, but rejoices in giving to those who can't.

Love bears all things, believes all things, hopes all things, and endures all things.

Love never fails. Video games will break; necklaces will be lost; golf clubs will rust; but *giving the gift of love will endure.*[2]

*Love is the
greatest thing in the world*
and the most important
ingredient in life.

Liberate your love.

Spread it out.

Keep giving it away.

Don't mind if

you *overflow* with it.

If there is damage done

it is easily repaired!

George Matthew Adams

My idea of Christmas,

whether old-fashioned or modern,

is very simple: *loving others.*

Come to think of it,

why do we have to wait for Christmas

to do that?

Bob Hope

Love seeks not itself to please,

Nor for itself has any care,

But for another gives its ease,

And *builds a heaven in hell's despair.*

William Blake

FRANCIS'S OYSTER DRESSING

This is a delicious complement to your Christmas turkey.

Ingredients (for a 12- to 14-pound turkey):

1½ cups celery (chopped)

2 large onions (chopped)

¼ cup (½ stick) salted butter

1 bag (14 ounces) unseasoned bread crumbs

½ cup milk

2 eggs

Salt to taste

1 tsp. poultry seasoning

½ pint oysters (or more, as desired)

Instructions:

Sauté celery and onions in the butter in a large pan. Add the bread crumbs and mix. Add the milk. Mix. Add the eggs. Mix again. Remove from heat and add salt, poultry seasoning, and oysters. Oysters can be chopped in a food processor or added whole. Stuff the turkey. Once the turkey has been stuffed, refrigerate immediately until ready to put into the oven.[3]

To know that *God so loved us*

as to give us his Son for our

dearest Brother, has brought human affection

to its highest tide

on the day of that Brother's birth.

If God so loved us, *how can we help*

loving one another?

Maltbie Babcock

This is how much

God loved the world:

He gave his Son,

his one and **only Son.**

JOHN 3:16

Christmas, my child, *is love in action.*

Every time we love,

every time we give,

it's Christmas.

Dale Evans Rogers

Are you willing to believe that

love is the strongest thing

in the world—

stronger than hate,

stronger than evil,

stronger than death—

and that the blessed life

which began in Bethlehem

nineteen hundred years ago

is the image and brightness

of the Eternal Love?

Then you can keep

Christmas.

Henry Van Dyke

Christmas Is
JOY

My heart leaps for joy and I will give

thanks to him in song.

PSALM 28:7 NIV

CHRISTMAS IS JOY

"Good news of great joy for all the people"—that's how the Angel of the Lord announced the birth of Christ to humble shepherds watching their flocks in the fields. The long-awaited Messiah was here at last—the Savior who would bring to an end the reign of fear and death and reconcile all to their heavenly Father. "Go and see for yourselves," the Angel urged the shepherds. "The new King has just been born."

And so they went and found the child with His mother, Mary.

The lowly shepherds must have been amazed that God had chosen them to be part of such an auspicious event. Imagine their journey to Bethlehem, high with excitement, their hearts filled with joy as they quickly made their way to find the Holy Child, God's Son.

Does your heart swell with joy as you think about that extraordinary, world-changing, angel-filled night? When you really take hold of the "good news," you will never see Christmas in the same way again!

THE JOY YOU GIVE

Somehow, not only for Christmas,
but all the long year through,
The joy that you give to others
is the joy that comes back to you;
And the more you spend in blessing
the poor, the lonely, and sad,
The more to your heart's possessing,
Returns to make you glad,

John Greenleaf Whittier

You will live in joy and peace.

The mountains and hills will burst into song,

and the trees of the field will clap their hands!

Where once there were thorns, cypress trees will grow.

Where nettles grew, myrtles will sprout up.

These events will bring great honor to the LORD's name;

they will be an everlasting sign of his power and love.

Isaiah 55:12–13 NLT

The joy of *brightening* other lives, *bearing* each other's burdens, *easing* others' loads

and supplanting
empty hearts and lives
with *generous gifts*
becomes for us
the magic of
Christmas.

W. C. Jones

A SONG OF JOY AT DAWN

Paul Gerhardt
Translation by Catherine Winkworth

All my heart this night rejoices,
As I hear, far and near,
Sweetest angel voices;
"Christ is born," their choirs are singing,
Till the air, everywhere,
Now with joy is ringing.

For it dawns, the promised morrow
Of His birth, who the earth
Rescues from her sorrow.
God to wear our form descendeth,
Of His grace to our race
Here His Son He lendeth. . . .

Ye who pine in weary sadness,
Weep no more, for the door
Now is found of gladness.
Cling to Him, for He will guide you
Where no cross, pain or loss,
Can again betide you. . . .

Thee, dear Lord, with heed I'll cherish;
Live to Thee, and with Thee
Dying, shall not perish;
But shall dwell with Thee for ever,
Far on high, in the joy
That can alter never.

STAR OF BETHLEHEM COOKIES

Take these to the office to share with coworkers.

Ingredients:

1 cup granulated sugar

½ cup (1 stick) unsalted butter

1 tsp. salt

1⅔ cups all-purpose flour

1 tsp. baking powder

1 tsp. ground nutmeg

6 egg whites, stiffly beaten

Instructions:

Cream the sugar into the butter. Add the nutmeg and mix. In a separate bowl, add the salt and baking powder to the flour and mix well. Combine the butter mixture with the flour and mix well. Add the egg whites last. Chill dough. Roll out on floured board and cut with star cookie cutters. Bake at 375°F until lightly browned. When cool, decorate with blue and pink icing and silver sprinkles.

The soul of one who serves God

always *swims in joy,*

always *keeps holiday,*

and is always in the

mood for singing.

Saint John of the Cross

We are all
strings in the
*concert of
his joy.*

Jacob Böhme

There is no
greater joy than
knowing
Jesus!

Paul Medley

He who gives *joy*

to the world is

raised higher among men

than he who conquers the world.

Wilhelm Richard Wagner

JOY TO THE WORLD

Isaac Watts

Joy to the earth! The Savior reigns!
Let men their songs employ;
While fields and floods, rocks, hills and plains
Repeat the sounding joy,
Repeat the sounding joy,
Repeat, repeat the sounding joy.

AWAY IN A MANGER

Kathe Campbell

O ur donkeys had been invited to play themselves in three live nativity scenes—all on the same weekend. I wasn't the least surprised, and my husband, Ken, was tickled to pieces. With our family raised, it was as if he must hurry and live hard and fast before his oats and vinegar burned out. We did much in those days, riding or carting in parades, teaching kids to saddle and lope, or enlisting "Donk" to carry Jesus on His last ride every Palm Sunday at our church.

"Wonderful!" I eagerly agreed. "But have you given thought to the logistics of getting our crew to their appointed mangers on time? And I'll bet you forgot we're hosting the annual neighborhood Christmas party that same weekend."

As usual, my darlin's mouth had overshot his brain with his eternal, but lovable, donkey passions. "Why couldn't Mary have ridden to Bethlehem on a horse?" I irreverently mused.

As my words flew over his head and my redheaded tempest rose an octave, Ken yammered on. "Easy as pie. We'll load up Donk, Sam, Storm, and Sweet Pea as the understudy, and drop them off at the churches each evening. Our two students are really excited to help and will oversee children's rides at evening's end." I felt like an old Scrooge.

While Ken fervently pulled necessary strings, I peered out the window, reminiscing about Christmases past. Sunlit frosty crystals glittering like jewels hovered over our snowy fields, and comical snowmen graced every gate along our road. One week always left us in a minus-zero funk, but we took it in stride with the sun peeking out every now and then through brief arctic blasts. As twenty-eight-year mountaineers, the short milder days blessed us, and lest we suffer a fluke of Mother Nature, the minus fifties would never benumb our ranch again.

There's a lot to be said for living on a tranquil 7,000-foot forested mountain only twenty minutes from suburbia. We breathe in the scent of pine, fir, and cedar breezes, and listen to the sweet sounds of Rocky Mountain birds. Other than a pair of coyotes feigning their music together as though they numbered a half dozen, deafening quiet usually reigns. Now and then a moose or deer brings its young just yards from our deck and stays through the balmy days of summer.

It has been an ideal place to raise this herd of carefully bred mammoth donkeys. Not just any donkeys, for our midlife lunacy had spawned champion performers, four debuting in the national Versatility Hall of Fame.

With the crew semiretired, friends and relatives hastily query, "What are you guys going to do with them now?"

"Why, eat them, of course," Ken always retorts with a wink.

So we loaded them up and dropped them off with their halters, treats, and handlers. They were groomed nearly as meticulously as were the parishioners who took great care with their own beards and makeup. As we approached the nativity scene staged on the busy corner over a great expanse of yard beneath soft, muted lights, youngsters took delight in welcoming me and my famed donkey.

Costuming was just a tad fancier than the usual array of colorful scarves, men's bathrobes, and someone's old prom dress. Attire was lovingly and authentically crafted upon sewing machines, to be treasured and worn annually. A small light centered upon the boy Jesus in His bed of straw, and Mary's face shown radiant as she and Joseph received gifts of gold, frankincense, and myrrh. Traditional Christmas carols softly pierced the cold, and every half hour the actors traded costumes and places while I plied Donk with treats.

While warming myself with the actors in the church vestibule, I noted that the entire ensemble was braving freezing temperatures in bare feet and sandals. Giving their all seemed more important than ruining the scene in awkward and tacky snow boots. Suddenly, a young man hurried in, laughing so hard he could barely speak. "Come quick, Mrs. C. Ya gotta get a load of what that donkey of yours is up to."

Oh Lordy, I grimly speculated, *I hope he hasn't upended that lovely crèche and everyone in it.* My boy was hustling again, wagging his tongue up and down, shaking hooves with the wise men, begging for seconds, keeping the crowd in stitches. I opened the back of the big square tent, pulled on his tail, and barked, "Knock it off, Donk! For a change you're not the star of this show!" Shortly thereafter, the sheep barreled over bales of straw into the crowded sidewalk, allowing eager younger shepherds to tend the flock around the perimeter.

And so it was, year after year, a major part of our city's Christmas celebrations with cameras snapping and the television stations and newspapers doing interviews. The other churches fared well with only minor calamities and equally large crowds clamoring for photo ops. After the audiences returned home, our donkey crew was happy to stretch their legs. I couldn't help but think the Christ Child was happy to know that a donkey that carried His mother was carrying joyful children in honor of His birth.[4]

HOLIDAY FRUIT FIZZ

Ho! Ho! Ho!

Ingredients:

1 can (12 ounces) frozen
  orange juice concentrate

1 cup lemon juice

1½ cups sugar

1–2 liters ginger ale, or
  citrus-flavored soft drink

Ice cubes

Instructions:

Mix thawed orange juice with lemon juice and sugar in a large
punch bowl. Stir until dissolved. Add ginger ale or citrus-flavored
soft drink slowly, stirring constantly. Add ice cubes.

I will praise you, LORD, with all my heart;

I will tell of all the marvelous things you have done.

I will be filled with joy because of you.

I will sing praises to your name, O Most High.

PSALM 9:1-2 NLT

AS WITH GLADNESS, MEN OF OLD

William Chatterton Dix

As with gladness, men of old
Did the guiding star behold;
As with joy they hailed its light,
Leading onward, beaming bright . . .

As with joyful steps they sped
To that lowly manger-bed,
There to bend the knee before
Him whom heav'n and earth adore . . .

As they offered gifts most rare
At that manger rude and bare;
So may we, with holy joy,
Pure, and free from sin's alloy,
All our costliest treasures bring,
Christ, to Thee, our heav'nly King.

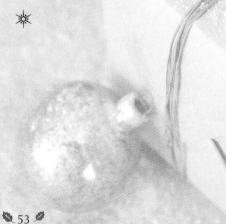

Warning . . . Warning . . . Warning!

ADVENT VIRUS

Author Unknown

Be on the alert for symptoms of inner **Hope**, **Peace**, **Joy**, and **Love**. The hearts of a great many have already been exposed to this virus, and it is possible that people everywhere could come down with it in epidemic proportions. This could pose a serious threat to what has, up to now, been a fairly stable condition of conflict in the world.

Signs to watch for . . .

1. A tendency to think and act spontaneously rather than on fears based on past experiences.

2. An unmistakable ability to enjoy each moment.

3. A loss of interest in judging other people.

4. A loss of interest in interpreting the actions of others.

5. A loss of interest in conflict.

6. A loss of the ability to worry (very serious).

7. Frequent, overwhelming episodes of appreciation.

8. Attacks of inexplicable smiling.

9. An increasing tendency to *let* things happen rather than *make* them happen.

10. An increased susceptibility to the love extended by others as well as the uncontrollable urge to extend it.

PLEASE PASS THIS WARNING ON TO YOUR FRIENDS AND FAMILY MEMBERS!

CHRISTMAS EVE

Martin Luther
Translated by Catherine Winkworth

Ah, dearest Jesus, holy Child,
Make Thee a bed, soft, undefiled,
Within my heart, that it may be
A quiet chamber kept for Thee.

My heart for very joy doth leap,
My lips no more can silence keep;
I too must sing with joyful tongue
That sweetest ancient cradle song—

Glory to God in highest Heaven,
Who unto man His Son hath given!
While angels sing with pious mirth
A glad new year to all the earth.

Christmas Is FAITH

Faith means being sure of the things

we hope for and knowing that something is

real even if we do not see it.

HEBREWS 11:1 NCV

CHRISTMAS IS FAITH

Christmas has faith written all over it. It's there in the song of Mary, a young woman who has never given herself to a man yet finds herself carrying a child. It's there in the words of Joseph as he announces he will take Mary as his wife, despite her condition. It's there in the actions of the shepherds who left their beloved flocks to seek the Christ Child. It's there in the hearts of the wise men as they follow a star to a faraway land in search of the One who would fulfill the Scriptures.

Faith permeates the story of the Nativity. It surrounds it and serves as the substance that holds all its various parts together.

This Christmas, take hold of the Christmas story with renewed faith. Apply it—to your words, as the shepherds did—to your actions, as the wise men did—to your heart, as Joseph did. Let your faith in the message of God's love for you, and the person of the Holy One who came to deliver that message, cause you to lift your voice in praise to God—just as Mary did!

God grant you the light in Christmas,
which is faith;

the warmth of Christmas,
which is love;

the radiance of Christmas,
which is purity;

the righteousness of Christmas,
which is justice;

the belief in Christmas,
which is truth;

the all of Christmas,
which is Christ.

Wilda English

These [signs] are written down
so you will believe that
Jesus is the Messiah, the Son of God,
and in the act of believing,
have *real and eternal life*
in the way he personally revealed it.

JOHN 20:31

CELESTIAL CARAMEL CORN

Ingredients:

Enough popped
   popping corn to
   make 6 quarts

1 cup (2 sticks) salted butter

2 cups brown sugar,
   firmly packed

½ cup corn syrup

1 tsp. salt

1 tsp. vanilla extract

½ tsp. baking soda

Instructions:

Preheat oven to 250°F. Butter the bottom and sides of a large broiler pan. Pop the popcorn and distribute the six quarts evenly in the pan. Melt butter in a saucepan. Add brown sugar, corn syrup, and salt and stir. Bring to a rolling boil, stirring constantly. Let boil without stirring for an additional 5 minutes. Remove from heat and add the vanilla, then the baking soda. Carefully pour the hot mixture over the popcorn as evenly as possible.

Bake for 1 hour, removing the pan from the oven every 15 minutes and stirring the popcorn. The warm coating should eventually coat all the popcorn. Remove from the oven and cool completely. Break apart and store in a tightly covered container.

Every tomorrow has two handles.

We can take hold of it

with the handle of anxiety

or the *handle of faith.*

Henry Ward Beecher

"THE TWELVE DAYS OF CHRISTMAS"
An Inspirational Adaptation

Author Unknown

- The "true love" represented God.

- The "partridge in a pear tree" represented Christ.

- The "two turtledoves" represented the Old and New Testaments of the Bible.

- The "three French hens" represented faith, hope, and charity.

- The "four calling birds" represented the four Gospels: Matthew, Mark, Luke, and John.

- The "five golden rings" represented the Pentateuch: the first five books of the Bible.

- The "six geese a-laying" represented the six days of Creation.

- The "seven swans a-swimming" represented the seven gifts of the Holy Spirit.

- The "eight maids a-milking" represented the eight beatitudes.

- The "nine ladies dancing" represented the nine fruit of the Holy Spirit.

- The "ten lords a-leaping" represented the Ten Commandments.

- The "eleven pipers piping" represented the eleven faithful apostles.

- The "twelve drummers drumming" represented the twelve points of doctrine in the Apostles' Creed.

A CHRISTMAS FOR JULIE

Nancy Julien Kopp

Painful Christmases etch themselves into our hearts and minds, never to be forgotten. Difficult holiday times, which cut into the soul, linger in our memories and are brought soaring back when we least expect them. A picture, a song, or a phrase triggers that which we thought remained locked safely away.

One such Christmas continues to haunt me, while at the same time surrounds me with the love and peace transcended by the Christmas story of Jesus' birth.

Forty-one years ago, my husband and I were new parents. Our baby girl was born a few days after Thanksgiving, bringing us both great joy and bottomless sorrow. Unlike today, no sonogram had prepared us for the news that Julie was a spina bifida baby. Because of a large opening in her spine, she was paralyzed from the waist down—legs, bowels, and bladder. Numb with shock, we agreed to the pediatrician's suggestion to transfer her to a renowned children's hospital in Chicago, an hour from our home.

"You can take her there as soon as we get the paperwork done," he told us.

With heavy hearts, we drove on icy roads from our home in a small Illinois town to the center of the big city on Lake Michigan. I held Julie close and gazed at her sweet face peeking out of a soft pink blanket. When we arrived at the hospital, a paperwork snafu in the Admissions Department gave us four more precious hours to hold and feed her. It turned out to be a most precious gift.

Our footsteps echoed in the wide hallway as we finally carried her to the fourth floor. A nurse with a sympathetic smile gently lifted our tiny daughter from my arms and carried her through the nursery door. I will never forget the ache of my empty arms or the slow breaking of my heart at that moment. My husband's hand clasped mine during our walk downstairs as we prepared to face an uncertain future.

It was the first of many trips to the hospital where we spent special moments with our baby girl, consulted with doctors, and attempted to ease our sorrow. We grasped each piece of good news and held on tightly. We crumbled a little more whenever a doctor delivered a grim outlook for our child—multiple surgeries, a life of probable infections, wheelchair, crutches, and other unknowns. Only faith kept us from screaming in denial when hearing the dire predictions. Only faith brought back our strength after discussing the future with Julie's doctors.

December arrived, and each time we visited, I noted more signs of the season. Garland, ribbons, and bows were strung throughout the halls. The waiting rooms had tiny Christmas trees, and some of the nurses wore Christmas pins on their uniforms.

One Sunday afternoon when we arrived at our station outside the nursery window, we could not help but smile. A small doll was tied onto Julie's tiny crib with a cheery red ribbon. No wings, but she reminded me of a guardian angel as she seemed to watch over our child. We questioned the nurse about the doll. Where had it come from? Who gave it to her?

"The auxiliary ladies bring a gift to every child in the hospital at Christmastime," she said. "They're the same wonderful women who come and rock the babies because we don't have time."

Unlike today, hospital rules kept us from being close enough to touch our baby, but a stranger had rocked her in our place, and another had brought her first Christmas gift. I could not help but think of Mary in the stable holding her child close and rocking Him in her arms as He received the first Christmas gifts from the wise men who had followed the star.

Each time we returned during that December, I checked to be sure Julie's gift remained tied to her crib. Was it my imagination, or did that doll glow? We talked to other parents who had children on the same floor. Children with heart problems, severe malformations, muscular weakness, and more—our children shared the same home this Christmas. Our hearts were not the only ones breaking during this season of love and joy.

Christmas morning found us on the road to the hospital once more. Again we stood outside the nursery window adoring our daughter with our eyes, while that empty-arms feeling washed over me again. She had been placed on her tummy to protect the surgical site on her spine. Christmas music played softly in the background. Julie lifted her silver-blonde head and turned toward us, one eye open, tiny hands clenched into fists. "Merry Christmas, Darling Girl," I whispered. My husband's arm slipped around me. Other parents moved through the halls spending Christmas morning with their little ones, too.

It was Julie's only Christmas, but it was one filled with the love of those who cared for her, family and friends in a small community who prayed for her, and the lifetime of love we bestowed on her during her few weeks on earth. To me, that's what Christmas is all about. Love and giving and a special glow from a tiny doll with a red ribbon around her tummy remain a part of my memory of that very special Christmas for Julie.[5]

It would be easy to dismiss Christmas as wholly secular

when we look around and see nothing but garish

commercialization and wanton appeals to selfishness and

greed. It is up to us to remember the true meaning

of Christmas. God clothed his son, Jesus, in

mortal flesh and sent him to be born in

the way of human beings and live among

us. *We must not forget the incarnation,*

for it defines for us the heart of God.

What kindness, what generosity, what selfless love. When you feel the winds

of Christmas swirling around

you, pause for a moment and

speak a prayer of grateful praise.

It will help you keep things in

perspective.

Andrea Garney

CHRISTMAS COLLECTIVE PRAYER

Adapted from the *Book of Common Prayer*

O God, who makes us glad with the yearly remembrance of the birth of Your only Son Jesus Christ, grant that as we joyfully receive Him as our Redeemer, so we may with sure confidence behold Him when He shall come to be our Judge, who lives and reigns with You and the Holy Ghost, one God, world without end.

O God, who hast caused this holy night to shine with the illumination of the true Light, grant us, we beseech You, that as we have known the

mystery of that Light upon earth, so may we also perfectly enjoy Him in heaven; where with You and the Holy Spirit He lives and reigns, one God, in glory everlasting.

Almighty God, who hast given us Your only-begotten Son to take our nature upon Him, and as at this time to be born of a pure virgin, grant that we, who have been born again and made Your children by adoption and grace, may daily be renewed by Your Holy Spirit, through our Lord Jesus Christ, to whom with You and the same Spirit be honor and glory, now and forever. **Amen.**

THE COBBLER'S GUEST

Author Unknown

There once lived in the city of Marseilles an old shoemaker, loved and honored by his neighbors, who affectionately called him "Father Martin."

One Christmas Eve, as he sat alone in his little shop reading of the visit of the wise men to the infant Jesus, and of the gifts they brought, he said to himself, "If tomorrow were the first Christmas, and if Jesus were to be born in Marseilles this night, I know what I would give Him!" He rose from his stool and took from a shelf overhead two tiny shoes of softest snow-white leather, with bright silver buckles. "I would give Him those, my finest work."

Replacing the shoes, he blew out the candle and retired to rest. Hardly had he closed his eyes, it seemed, when he heard a voice call his name . . . "Martin! Martin!"

Intuitively he felt a presence. Then the voice spoke again . . . "Martin, you have wished to see Me. Tomorrow I shall pass by your window. If you see Me, and bid Me enter, I shall be your guest at your table."

Father Martin did not sleep that night for joy. And before it was yet dawn he rose and swept and tidied up his little shop. He spread fresh sand upon the floor, and wreathed green boughs of fir along the rafters. On the spotless linen-covered table he placed a loaf of white bread, a jar of honey, and a pitcher of milk, and over the fire he hung a pot of tea. Then he took up his patient vigil at the window.

Presently he saw an old street-sweeper pass by, blowing upon his thin, gnarled hands to warm them. "Poor fellow, he must be half frozen," thought Martin. Opening the door he called out to him, "Come in, my friend, and warm, and drink a cup of hot tea." And the man gratefully accepted the invitation.

An hour passed, and Martin saw a young, miserably clothed woman carrying a baby. She paused wearily to rest in the shelter of his doorway. The heart of the old cobbler was touched. Quickly he flung open the door.

"Come in and warm while you rest," he said to her. "You do not look well," he remarked.

"I am going to the hospital. I hope they will take me in, and my baby boy," she explained. "My husband is at sea, and I am ill, without a soul."

"Poor child!" cried Father Martin. "You must eat something while you are getting warm. No. Then let me give a cup of milk to the little one. Ah! What a bright, pretty fellow he is! Why, you have put no shoes on him!"

"I have no shoes for him," sighed the mother sadly. "Then he shall have this lovely pair I finished yesterday." And Father Martin took down from the shelf the soft little snow-white shoes he had admired the evening be-fore. He slipped them on the child's feet . . . they fit perfectly. And shortly the young mother left, two shoes in her hand and tearful with gratitude.

And Father Martin resumed his post at the window. Hour after hour went by, and although many people passed his window, and many needy souls shared his hospitality, the expected Guest did not appear.

"It was only a dream," he sighed, with a heavy heart. "I did believe; but He has not come."

Suddenly, so it seemed to his weary eyes, the room was flooded with a strange light. And to the cobbler's astonished vision there appeared before him, one by one, the poor street-sweeper, the sick mother and her child, and all the people whom he had aided during the day. And each smiled at him and said, "Have you not seen Me? Did I not sit at your table?" Then they vanished.

At last, out of the silence, Father Martin heard again the gentle voice repeating the old familiar words, "Whoever welcomes one of these little children in My name welcomes Me; and whoever welcomes Me does not welcome Me but the one who sent Me." . . . "I was hungry and you gave Me something to eat, I was thirsty and you gave Me something to drink, I was a stranger and you invited Me in, I needed clothes and you clothed Me, I was sick and you looked after Me, I was in prison and you came to visit Me."

*Faith is
the sight of the
inward eye.*

Alexander MacLaren

THE TEN COMMANDMENTS OF CHRISTMAS

Paul Ciniraj

I. Thou shalt not leave "Christ" out of Christmas.

II. Thou shalt not value thy gifts by the cost, for many shall signify love that is more blessed and beautiful than silver and gold.

III. Thou shalt give thyself with thy gifts, thy love, thy personality, and thy service and shalt increase the value of thy gifts a hundred fold, and they who receiveth them shall treasure them forever.

IV. Thou shalt not let Santa Claus take the place of Christ, lest Christmas become a fairy tale, rather than a sublime reality in the spiritual realm.

V. Thou shalt not burden thy servants, the salesgirl, the mail carrier and the merchant.

VI. Thou shalt not neglect the church. Its Christmas services are planned to help spiritualize the Christmas season for thee, thy family, and thy friends.

VII. Thou shalt not neglect the needy. Let thy bountiful blessings be shared with the many who will go hungry and cold unless you are generous at Christmas.

VIII. Thou shalt be as a little child. Christmas is the day of the Christ child; not until thou has become, in spirit, as a little child art thou ready to enter into the Kingdom of heaven.

IX. Thou shalt prepare thy soul for Christmas. Verily, most of us spend much time and money getting gifts ready, but few seconds in preparing our souls.

X. Thou shalt give thy heart to Christ. Let thy Christmas list have "Christ in my heart" at the top as thy gift to Him this Christmas.[6]

The way to Christmas lies through

an ancient gate. . . .

It is a little gate, child-high, child-wide,

and there is a password:

"Peace on earth to men of good will."

May you, this Christmas,

become as a little child again

and enter into His kingdom.

Angelo Patri

For to us a child is born,

to us a son is given,

and the government will be on his shoulders.

And he will be called

Wonderful Counselor, Mighty God,

Everlasting Father, Prince of Peace.

Of the increase of his government and peace

there will be no end.

Isaiah 9:6–7 NIV

Christmas Is
PEACE

Suddenly a great company of the heavenly host appeared with the angel, praising God and saying, "Glory to God in the highest, and on earth peace to men on whom his favor rests."

LUKE 2:13–14 NIV

CHRISTMAS IS PEACE

Jesus was born into a world of great conflict. For generations before His birth and generations after His death, peace simply did not exist. Yet the angels called Him the Prince of Peace.

However, during His time on earth, Jesus was not the prince of an earthly kingdom, but rather of the Kingdom of God. He came to bring peace to our hearts rather than peace to the nations. His mission was to bring an endless peace between God the Father and His fallen creation—one rebellious heart at a time.

As you celebrate Christmas, may you not allow this season with its drop-dead schedules, endless list of tasks, and checkbook-straining costs to steal your peace of mind and heart. In the midst of it all, allow God's peace to emerge—peace that passes human understanding, peace that comes from knowing that when you receive God's gift, you are God's beloved child, redeemed and reconciled, and a recipient of the greatest gift ever given.

When the song of the angels is stilled,

When the star in the sky is gone,

When the kings and princes are home,

When the shepherds are back with their flock,

The work of Christmas begins:

To find the lost, To heal the broken,
To feed the hungry, To release the prisoner,
To rebuild the nations, To bring peace among others,
To make music in the heart.

Howard Thurman

SILENT NIGHT! HOLY NIGHT!

Josef Mohr

Translated by John Freeman Young

Silent night! Holy night!
All is calm, all is bright
'Round yon virgin mother and Child.
Holy Infant so tender and mild,
Sleep in heavenly peace,
Sleep in heavenly peace. . . .

Silent night! Holy night!
All is dark, save the light
Yonder, where they sweet vigil keep,
O'er the Babe who in silent sleep
Rests in heavenly peace,
Rests in heavenly peace.

THE ANGEL AND THE SHEPHERDS

Lew Wallace

A mile and a half, it may be two miles, southeast of Bethlehem, there is a plain separated from the town by an intervening swell of the mountain. . . .

At the side farthest from the town, close under a bluff, there was an extensive *mârâh*, or sheepcot, ages old. In some long-forgotten foray, the building had been unroofed and almost demolished. The enclosure attached to it remained intact, however, and that was of more importance to the shepherds who drove their charges thither than the house itself. . . .

There were six of these men, omitting the watchman; and afterwhile they assembled in a group near the fire, some sitting, some lying prone. . . .

They rested and talked; and their talk was all about their flocks, a dull theme to the world, yet a theme which was all the world to them. . . .

While they talked, and before the first watch was over, one by one the shepherds went to sleep, each lying where he had sat.

The night, like most nights of the winter season in the hill country, was clear, crisp, and sparkling with stars. There was no wind. The atmosphere seemed never so pure, and the stillness was more than silence; it was a holy hush, a warning that heaven was stooping low to whisper some good thing to the listening earth.

By the gate, hugging his mantle close, the watchman walked; at times he stopped, attracted by a stir among the sleeping herds, or by a jackal's cry off on the mountain-side. The midnight was slow in coming to him; but at last it came. His task was done; now for the dreamless sleep with which labor blesses its wearied children! He moved towards the fire, but paused; a light was breaking around him, soft and white, like the moon's. He waited breathlessly. The light deepened; things before invisible came to view; he saw the whole field, and all it sheltered. A chill sharper than that of the frosty air—a chill of fear—smote him. He looked up; the stars were gone; the light was dropping as from a window in the sky; as he looked, it became a splendor; then, in terror, he cried,

"Awake, awake!"

Up sprang the dogs, and, howling, ran away.

The herds rushed together bewildered.

The men clambered to their feet, weapons in hand.

"What is it?" they asked, in one voice.

"See!" cried the watchman, "the sky is on fire!"

Suddenly the light became intolerably bright, and they covered their eyes, and dropped upon their knees; then, as their souls shrank with fear, they fell upon their faces blind and fainting, and would have died had not a voice said to them:

"Fear not!"

And they listened.

"Fear not: for behold, I bring you good tidings of great joy, which shall be to all people."

The voice, in sweetness and soothing more than human, and low and clear, penetrated all their being, and filled them with assurance. They rose upon their knees, and, looking worshipfully, beheld in the center of a great glory the appearance of a man, clad in a robe intensely white; above its shoulders towered the tops of wings shining and folded; a star over its forehead glowed with steady luster, brilliant as Hesperus; its hands were stretched towards them in blessing; its face was serene and divinely beautiful. . . .

The herald spoke not again; his good tidings were told; yet he stayed awhile. Suddenly the light, of which he seemed the center, turned roseate and began to tremble; then up, as far as the men could see, there was a flashing of white wings, and coming and going of radiant forms, and voices as of a multitude chanting in unison,

"Glory to God in the highest, and on earth, peace, good-will towards men!"

When the shepherds came fully to their senses, they stared at each other stupidly, until one of them said, "It was Gabriel, the Lord's messenger unto men." . . .

[One shepherd] gazed into the fire thoughtfully, but at length said, like one possessed of a sudden resolve, "There is but one place in Bethlehem where there are mangers; but one, and that is the cave near the old khan. Brethren, let us go see this thing which has come to pass. The priests and doctors have been a long time looking for the Christ. Now he is born, and the Lord has given us a sign by which to know him. Let us go up and worship him." . . .

They were led to one of the mangers, and there the child was. The lantern was brought, and the shepherds stood by mute. The little one made no sign; it was as others just born. . . .

And the simple men, never doubting, kissed the hem of the mother's robe, and with joyful faces departed. In the khan, to all the people aroused and pressing about them, they told their story; and through the town, and all the way back to the *mârâh*, they chanted the refrain of the angels, "Glory to God in the highest, and on earth peace, good-will towards men!" . . .

HOLIDAY EGGNOG

This drink will bring warmth to your body and peace to your soul.

Ingredients:

12 large eggs

1¼ cups sugar

½ tsp. salt

2 quarts whole milk

2 Tbsp. vanilla extract

1 tsp. ground nutmeg

1 cup heavy cream

Instructions:

In a heavy 4-quart saucepan beat eggs, sugar, and salt with a wire whisk until blended. Gradually stir in 1 quart of the milk and cook over low heat. Stir constantly until the mixture thickens and coats the back of a spoon (about 25 minutes). Do not boil.

Pour the mixture into a large bowl and add the vanilla extract, nutmeg, and remaining quart of milk. Beat the cream until soft peaks form. Fold into the cooked mixture with the whisk. Pour into a chilled punch bowl and sprinkle with additional nutmeg.

There's more, much more, to Christmas

Than candlelight and cheer;

It's the spirit of sweet friendship

That brightens all year.

It's thoughtfulness and kindness.

It's hope reborn again.

For peace, for understanding,

And for goodwill to men!

Author Unknown

To cherish peace
and goodwill,

to be plenteous
in mercy,
is to have the

real spirit
of Christmas.

THE ANGEL'S SONG

Carol from the Middle Ages
Author Unknown

Now let us sing the Angel's song

That rang so sweet and clear,

When heav'nly light and music fell

on earthly eye and ear;

To Him we sing, our Savior King,

Who always deigns to hear:

"Glory to God, and peace on earth." . . .

He came to bring a glorious gift,

Good will to men—and why?

Because He loved us, Jesus came

For us to live and die;

Then sweet and long, the Angel's song,

Again we raise on high.

"Glory to God, and peace on earth."

A REFUGEE CAMP CHRISTMAS

Renie Burghardt

During World War II, we had many sad Christmases. Fear was always lurking in some nearby corner. Those were the times we mainly observed Christmas in our hearts. So when in 1947, we arrived in the refugee camp in Austria, just a few weeks before Christmas, I wasn't expecting anything different. At age eleven, I had become resigned to not having much.

The refugee camp, with its wooden barracks and dusty lanes, was pretty drab. But we had a warm place to sleep, warm food to eat, and were outfitted with warm clothes donated to the refugee effort from various generous-minded countries like the United States, Canada, and Great Britain. So we considered ourselves pretty fortunate. And we had some of the most beautiful views available, free to anyone who wished to look, since the camp was located in one of the most scenic areas of Austria-Carinthia.

As Christmas was approaching, the refugee camp school I attended made plans to help us celebrate the holiday as a group. In the barracks we lived in, our private spaces were tiny cubicles where we slept. There was no room for individual celebrations. But the school had a large auditorium, where a donated Christmas tree was set up, which we, the children, helped decorate with our own handmade ornaments. There were candles on the tree, too, which were to be lit on Christmas Eve, just like it used to be done in Hungary, before the war. And we were rehearsing the school Christmas play, to be presented on Christmas Eve. I had a small part in the play, as the angel who comes to give the message to the shepherds about the birth of the Savior. I was very pleased and excited about the part.

On Christmas Eve afternoon, my grandparents and I decided to take a walk to the small town of Spittal, just a few miles from the camp. Grandfather felt that even though we had no money to buy anything, taking in the Christmas sights and smells would be worth the walk. The town's cobbled streets, with its many small shops, were decorated with fir branches, and small trees in shopwindows glowed with lit candles. People were hustling and bustling, getting last-minute things for the holiday, and wishing each other "*Fröhliche Weihnachten.*" We stopped in front of the bakery and inhaled the delicious smells coming out of it every time someone opened the door. I gazed at the Napoleons, displayed in the window, my mouth watering. "Oh, they must taste so delicious," I said wistfully.

"And that poppy seed kalacs (*kuchen*) looks wonderful, too," Grandmother sighed.

"Maybe this wasn't such a good idea," Grandfather said. "Now everyone is hungry for something they cannot have!" He sounded very sad.

"But who is to say that you cannot have a Napoleon, or some of that poppy seed kuchen?" a voice behind us asked, as a woman in a fur coat and hat took my hand. "Come on, let us all go into the bakery."

"Oh, no!" I protested, trying to pull my hand out of hers. But she wouldn't let go, and inside the bakery, bought a large Napoleon square and some kuchen, just for us. "Froliche Weinachten," she called out merrily, and then disappeared into a crowd of people. A Christmas angel in a fur coat!

On the way back to the refugee camp, as I sank my teeth into that delicious, custard-filled Napoleon, and got powdered sugar all over myself, I was already happy. But there were more wonderful surprises ahead.

That evening, Christmas Eve, they lit the candles on the community Christmas tree, and all the adults came to watch our Christmas play, which went off very nicely. Everyone remembered their lines, the choir sang some beautiful, Hungarian Christmas songs, and people had tears in their eyes. Then the presents were handed out, for, yes indeed, there were presents for all the kids under that tree.

When I opened mine, I found a pair of red, fuzzy mittens and a matching scarf in the box, and inside one of the mittens, there was a little note, written in English. "Merry Christmas from Mary Anne, in Buffalo, New York, United States of America." Imagine that, a gift from a girl all the way in America! I wondered later how old she was, what she looked like, what she liked to do, as I tried to fall asleep while my imagination kept working overtime.

When I awoke on Christmas morning, it was already light out, and there were noises coming through the thin, wooden boards of the barrack.

"Good morning, sweetheart. Merry Christmas," Grandmother said.

"Why is there so much noise out there already?" I asked sleepily, rubbing my eyes.

"Well, I guess some early-rising children are enjoying all the newly fallen snow."

"Oh, did it snow overnight?" I said, leaping from the cot and reaching for some warm clothes to put on. "How wonderful! And where is Grandfather?"

"He and some of the other men are shoveling some paths, so people can go for their breakfast, and to church."

Within seconds, I was out there, too, marveling at nature's power to turn a drab refugee camp into a pristine, winter wonderland!

Soon, the surrounding snow-covered hills were filled with squealing

Austrian children, sledding down those hills in their new Christmas sleds, or shushing down on their new skis, while refugee camp children built snowmen, had snowball fights, and made snow angels, squealing with just as much delight. Nature's gift of snow was free for everyone to enjoy!

Later, as I gazed at the snow-covered mountains, with their majestic, snow-dusted spruce trees, so breathtakingly beautiful, my heart filled with peace and joy, and with tears in my eyes, I thanked God for a wonderful Christmas. Even though we were far from home, we were surrounded by loved ones and the love and generosity of others—some perfect strangers. I knew it was a Christmas I would never forget.[7]

Christmas began in the *heart of God.*
It is complete only when
it reaches the *heart of man.*

Author Unknown

IT CAME UPON THE MIDNIGHT CLEAR

Edmund Hamilton Sears

It came upon the midnight clear
That glorious song of old,
From angels bending near the earth
To touch their harps of gold:
"Peace to the earth, goodwill to men
From heaven's all-gracious King!"
The world in solemn stillness lay
To hear the angels sing. . . .

For lo! The days are hastening on,
By prophet-bards foretold,
When with the ever-circling years
Comes 'round the age of gold;
When peace shall over all the earth
Its ancient splendors fling,
And the whole world send back the song,
Which now the angels sing.

105

FROZEN MINT SALAD

This delightful salad will make your holiday table extra special.

Ingredients:

- 1 can (20 ounces) pineapple chunks (with juice)
- 1 can (8 ounces) pineapple chunks (with juice)
- 1 package lime Jell-O
- 1 cup butter mints, crushed
- 1 cup miniature marshmallows
- 1 carton (8 ounces) whipped topping

Instructions:

Pour the pineapple into a large bowl. Do NOT drain. Add the Jell-O powder. Stir until the Jell-O is mixed well with the pineapple. Add 2/3 of the butter mints and all the marshmallows. Mix well. Add the whipped topping and mix well. Put into molds and freeze. Garnish with the remainder of the crushed butter mints.

Blow, bugles of battle, the marches of peace;

East, west, north, and south let the long quarrel cease;

Sing the song of great joy that the angels began,

Sing of glory to God and of good-will to man!

John Greenleaf Whittier

CHRISTMAS BELLS

Henry Wadsworth Longfellow

I heard the bells on Christmas day
Their old, familiar carols play,
And wild and sweet
The words repeat
Of peace on earth, good will to men!

And thought how, as the day had come,
The belfries of all Christendom
Had rolled along
The unbroken song
Of peace on earth, good will to men!

And in despair I bowed my head;
"There is no peace on earth," I said;
"For hate is strong,
And mocks the song
Of peace on earth, good will to men!"

Then pealed the bells more loud and deep;
"God is not dead; nor does He sleep!
The wrong shall fail
The right prevail,
With peace on earth, good will to men!"

Till, ringing, singing on its way
The world revolved from night to day,
A voice, a chime,
A chant sublime
Of peace on earth, good will to men!

Peace on earth

will come to stay,

When we live

Christmas every day.

Helen Steiner Rice

Like a bell,

    with solemn, sweet vibrations,

I hear once more the voice

    of Christ say *"Peace!"*

Henry Wadsworth Longfellow

Christmas Is FUN

Our mouths were filled with laughter,

our tongues with songs of joy.

PSALM 126:2 NIV

CHRISTMAS IS FUN

At Christmas we celebrate the birth of Christ, the Messiah, the Savior, the Redeemer. Who could walk around with a glum face when the light of God is shining full and free into hearts and lives? It is, after all, the greatest, most exciting, most fabulous miracle of love that has ever happened. That little babe lying in a manger bed brought with Him from Heaven a new beginning, a fresh start for every man, woman, and child on earth. Even the memory of such an event is reason to laugh and sing and make merry.

Don't hold back, child of God. Be of good humor. Exercise your funny bone! God takes pleasure in your laughter, just as much as He cares about your tears. He tells us in His Word that it's good for your body and good for your soul. It can help you avoid sickness and gain perspective. Give yourself permission to celebrate Christmas this year—really celebrate, and have a knee-slappin', eye-waterin', belly-laughin' good time.

Perhaps the best

Yuletide

decoration

is being

wreathed in

smiles.

Author Unknown

THE ROBE LESS TRAVELED

Todd and Jedd Hafer

Christmastime at Broomfield Baptist Church always means one thing: The Annual All-Church Christmas Program, also known as "The Poorly Contrived Debacle with Barely Tolerable Music."

One particularly memorable year, Betty Eunice, the choir director, decided to produce a program titled *Away in a Manger*. On November first, she proudly and carefully arranged the letters on our outdoor sign. We assumed she wanted to give people plenty of advance warning (oops, we mean notice) about the program.

Unfortunately, her foresight gave our brother Chadd too much time to stare at the sign:

> Come One, Come All
>
> To Broomfield Baptist Church's
>
> Christmas presentation of
>
> AWAY IN A MANGER!

After carefully evaluating the sign for a week, Chadd walked to the church late one night and removed an "A" and an "M" from the board.

Then he stood back to admire his work. AWAY IN A MANGER! was now AWAY IN ANGER!

The sign stayed that way until the morning of the program. We were sure Betty Eunice must not have seen the change, or someone would have experienced grief and woe of Old Testament proportions. As for the people who saw the NCV (New Chadd Version) sign, the title must have intrigued them because on that fateful December day Broomfield Baptist Church was packed to the rafters with an eager, standing-room-only crowd.

That year our dad was fortunate enough to be chosen to play the prophet Isaiah, a role that suited him to a T. His job in the program was to walk to the podium and foretell the Christmas story, wearing the robe fit for an Old Testament important person.

During the first three weeks of December, all the rest of the cast members worked diligently on their costumes, striving to achieve painstaking biblical/historical accuracy. They bejeweled their headdresses or togas, or whatever they call them, from authentic goat skin. (Well, it certainly *looked* authentic.)

As for our dad's preparation, well, let's just say the first three weeks of December comprised the crucial part of the National Football League season. Costumes were not part of his consciousness unless they had last names and numbers on them and belonged to the Denver Broncos.

However, to his credit, we must point out that Dad put several moments of thought into his costume as he rolled out of bed on the morning of the presentation. He shucked the pillowcase off his pillow and wrapped it around his head, securing it with his favorite tie (the blue and white checked number with the little yellow rocking horses). Then he gazed into his bedroom mirror and said, "Behold, an authentic Old Testament prophet turban!"

For the finishing touch, he threw on "the robe." The robe is famous in our family. Until that day, it was not famous beyond our family because Mom decreed that it was never (under any circumstances) to be worn outside the house.

The robe was olive-green (minus the pimento) and was certainly large enough to cover an adult male, as long as that male was a jockey. On a large former semiprofessional football player, the robe was like a tea cozy on a keg of root beer. We can only imagine the draft Dad felt when he stepped into the crisp December air and walked to the church that morning.

Betty Eunice nearly had a heart attack when she saw Dad waiting backstage.

"Pastor Hafer!" she gasped. "Where's your costume? And what is that thing on your head? Has one of your awful children played another joke on you?"

Dad frowned and adjusted his authentic pillowcase turban. "This *is* my costume," he announced, punctuating the words with his signature tone of pastoral authority. Poor Betty Eunice was decidedly outgunned.

"Oh, my! Oh, my! Oh, my!" said Betty Eunice, holding on to a cardboard ox for support.

Dad shrugged his massive shoulders, adjusted the mini-robe, and took his place at stage left (also known as the secretary's office).

A hush fell over the congregation as a crimson-faced Betty Eunice stepped to the microphone, fanning herself with a bulletin. "We are, uh, proud, to present to you, us, our Christmas program today. It's called *Away in a Manger.* God help us all."

Then she sat down in the front pew and began to weep softly.

Dad, taking that as his cue, emerged from stage left and thundered to the podium. Chadd held his breath. His new girlfriend, Sarah, had come all the way from Maryland to visit for Christmas. Her eyes grew as big as pies when she saw Dad's enormous tree-trunk thighs—almost all of them.

She leaned over and whispered to Chadd, "Hey, is that your dad or a retired member of the Power Team?"

Chadd's eyes were fixed on the major prophet before him. "Who?" he said absently.

"The huge guy in the little robe, Chadd! The guy reading from the scroll? Is that your dad?"

Chadd drew a long, slow breath. He looked Sarah directly in the eye. "No. No. That's not my dad. My dad is sick today. He's not here. He's not anywhere near here."

Somewhere, probably over at the Hanson farm, a rooster crowed.

Fortunately, Dad's part was over quickly. After the opening scene, he stepped down from the podium, tossed his scroll to Betty Eunice, and lumbered to the back of the sanctuary where Mom was frantically waving a T-shirt and an extra-large pair of sweatpants. Then he sat in a back pew and enjoyed the rest of the program. He even gave a solo standing ovation to Chet the elder after his tuba solo.

When the program was over (and the plastic baby Jesus was returned safely to the nursery, where he was known as G.I. Joe), the church began buzzing about the robe. A few of the elders teased Dad about his attire, saying that the real prophet Isaiah was probably taking some razzing in Heaven right about then.

"Hey, Pastor Del," Dave the elder said, "I'm glad your part didn't call for you to bend over. You woulda been arrested!"

Dad was unmoved by the chiding. He began to hold court in the fellowship area, explaining that his costume was authentic. "Old Testament prophets didn't make a lot of money," he noted. "They couldn't afford a lot of material for their clothes. Jeremiah, in fact, often wore nothing but a loincloth and calfskin knee brace."

The elders nodded in bewildered agreement. Chadd, however, was livid. "Hey, Dad," he said, "I have a prophecy for you: If you ever wear that robe in public again, me and the rest of the family are converting to another religion and moving to Idaho! Also, I told my new girlfriend you weren't my dad, so could you please not come home till she goes back to Maryland?"

Dad stared at Chadd. Then he picked up the robe, stuffed it into the pocket of his sweats, and went "away in anger."

Chadd and Dad eventually reconciled over the event, although Sarah took an early flight back to Maryland and never communicated with Chadd again.

And there were two more bits of fallout from that fateful Sunday. Betty Eunice decreed that from that point on, all Christmas programs were to be "non-prophet" affairs. But just to be on the safe side, Mom cut up the robe and made it into two oven mitts—rather small ones.[8]

WASSAIL

This recipe is great for warming the hearts of holiday carolers.

Ingredients:

2 quarts apple cider

2 cups orange juice

1 cup lemon juice

4 cups pineapple juice

1 cup sugar

3 cinnamon sticks

1 tsp. ground cloves

Instructions:

Combine all ingredients in a large container. Stir. Heat thoroughly but do not boil. Pour into a punch bowl and serve with a dipper, or use a coffeepot.

Laughter and a good sense of humor add *sweetness* to life's journey.

Paul Medley

Mirth is God's medicine.
Everybody ought to bathe in it.

Henry Ward Beecher

TWELVE SIGNS THIS YEAR'S HOLIDAY SEASON MIGHT BE A BUST!

1. You can't locate the Christmas cards and tree ornaments you bought last January for 75 percent off.

2. Neighborhood kids have been systematically taking out your Christmas lights with their BB guns.

3. You made the mistake of reading the list of chemicals injected into your holiday turkey!

4. You were the 622nd person in line for what turned out to be 621 Beach Ball Betty dolls.

5. You thought the gingerbread house in the center of your Aunt Velma's kitchen table was meant to be eaten and helped yourself.

6. Your Secret Santa opted out of the program early due to lack of interest—in you.

7. You promised your husband new transportation for Christmas before you realized he had his heart set on a Saab!

8. You saw an advertisement for reindeer meat in the window of your local supermarket.

9. When you and your family came to the door, the Christmas carolers stopped in mid-refrain and scurried over to the house next door.

10. You bought a magnificent seven-foot tree before you remembered your house has six-foot ceilings.

11. Blanche and Herbie are coming to your house for Christmas this year—and bringing the quints!

12. The local television station tracking Santa's sleigh announced it had disappeared from the radar.

O Evergreen, O Evergreen,

Your garb unfading shows,

O Evergreen, O Evergreen,

Your garb unfading shows,

The flow'r of joy about my door,

Good cheer that fails never more,

O Evergreen, O Evergreen,

My heart your lesson knows.

German Folk Song

Laughter is

the *spark* of the soul.

Author Unknown

Where do snowmen dance?

At a snowball

How do sheep greet each other at Christmas?

A merry Christmas to ewe!

What do snowman eat for breakfast?

Frosted flakes

What do snowmen wear on their heads?

Ice caps

What do you call a reindeer with ear muffs?

Anything you want—he can't hear you!

Be merry all, be merry all,

With holly dress and festive hall;

Prepare the song, the feast, the ball,

To *welcome merry*
Christmas.

William Robert Spencer

DECK THE HALLS

Deck the hall with boughs of holly,
Fa la la la la, la la la la.
'Tis the season to be jolly,
Fa la la la la, la la la la.

Don we now our gay apparel.
Fa la la la la, la la la la.
Troll the ancient Yuletide carol.
Fa la la la la, la la la la.

See the blazing Yule before us,
Fa la la la la, la la la la.
Strike the harp and join the chorus.
Fa la la la la, la la la la.

Follow me in merry measure,
Fa la la la la, la la la la.
While I tell the Yule tide treasure.
Fa la la la la, la la la la.

CHRISTMAS SONGS
FOR CATS

1. We Three Siamese

2. God Rest Ye Merry Alley Cats

3. Have Yourself a Merry Little Cat Nap

4. Up on the Countertop

5. I'm the Most Wonderful Cat of the Year

6. Claw the Walls

7. I'm Dreaming of a Big Fishy

8. It's Beginning to Look a Lot Like My Mouse

9. Frosty the Fat Cat

10. Climbing Around the Christmas Tree

CHRISTMAS SONGS FOR DOGS

1. All I Want for Christmas Is the Cat Next Door

2. Randolph the Brown-Nosed Rottweiler

3. Santa Claus Is Coming to the Pound

4. Do You Smell What I Smell?

5. The First Bow Wow

6. We Three Hounds of Orient Are

7. Jingle Tail Rock

8. Go Tell It at the Dog Park

9. What Bone Is This?

10. Jolly Old Saint Bernard

May each be found thus as the year circles round,

With mirth and good humor each Christmas be crowned,

And may all who have plenty of riches in store

With their bountiful blessings make happy the poor;

For never as yet it was counted a crime,

To be merry and cheery at that happy time.

Eighteenth Century Song
Author Unknown

A *person without a sense of humor* is like
a wagon without springs.
It's jolted by
every pebble on the road.

Henry Ward Beecher

Christmas Is
WONDER

Glorious and majestic are his deeds, and his

righteousness endures forever. He has caused

his wonders to be remembered.

PSALM 111:3–4 NIV

CHRISTMAS IS WONDER

Christmas at its core is larger than life, grander than we can begin to comprehend. We cannot even imagine the scenario—God, the Son, wrapping himself in human flesh and being born in a humble stable to parents of little worldly consequence. Perhaps that's why Christmas never loses its wonder year after year. The story simply cannot be taken in at once. It takes a lifetime of Christmases, and even then we remain starstruck, still unable to understand fully what God has done for us, what He has given us.

This Christmas, hold nothing back. Look up and hear the majestic angelic choir, look out into the night in search of the brilliant Christmas star. Cherish every expression of Christmas love, joy, and peace—immersing yourself in the wonder of it all! Don't worry about going overboard. In a million lifetimes, you could not grow weary of it—it's a truly eternal story.

As children, we lived in a world of wonder. The magic of a firefly in a canning jar. A litter of newborn kittens nestled close to their mother. Faraway adventures played out in the pages of a book. Clouds shaped like elephants and giraffes on a hot summer day. Peeking out the bedroom window on Christmas Eve in hope of seeing a gift-filled sleigh and eight reindeer parked on the snow-covered lawn. Yes, it's great to be a child. Before we toss all that wonder to the winds, however, let's remember that, as Christians, we are and will always be God's children. We should never lose our sense of the wonder we feel when we consider the gift of love He has given us through the birth of Christ—a gift that explodes with new life each and every day.

Trudy Truman

THE WONDER OF CHRISTMAS

D. V. Seigle

The wonder of Christmas is not found in

A mighty display of God's power,

But rather in the humility of God's love.

He didn't come as a ruling king, to crush our sin's rebellion.

Instead, He left the majesty of heaven

to become a helpless newborn babe,

so He could identify with our weakness and die for our sins.

A child has been born for us,

a son given to us;

authority rests upon his shoulders;

and he is named

Wonderful Counselor,

Mighty God,

Everlasting Father,

Prince of Peace.

ISAIAH 9:6 NRSV

WE THREE KINGS OF ORIENT ARE

John H. Hopkins Jr.

We three kings of Orient are;
Bearing gifts we traverse afar,
Field and fountain, moor and mountain,
Following yonder star.

O star of wonder, star of light,
Star with royal beauty bright,
Westward leading, still proceeding,
Guide us to thy perfect light.

May the
wonder that is
Christmas

touch the child

that is within

your heart.

Author Unknown

WHAT A WONDER

Marie Norton

A baby asleep in a manger
Yet He is the Savior of the world.
A man who drove merchandisers from the temple
Yet He willingly laid down His life for the same.
The King of all kings
Who came to die as a lamb.

The One who owned it all
Yet laid it all aside.
How can we explain such a man? We can't.
We must stand in awe and worship Him.

SNOW ICE CREAM

Making this treat is a wonderful way to delight your children on a snowy Christmas Day. (Make sure you get the snow from a clean, untouched area.)

Ingredients:

6 cups fresh snow

1 can (14 ounces)
   sweetened condensed milk

1 tsp. vanilla extract

Instructions:

Place a large pan or bowl outside to capture freshly fallen snow. Add the milk and the vanilla and stir. For a variation, add a can of root beer or cola. Ice cream melts very quickly, so serve immediately.

This is Christmas:

not the *tinsel,*

not the *giving and receiving,*

not even the *carols,*

but the **humble heart** that receives anew

the wondrous gift—the Christ.

Frank McKibben

A CHRISTMAS LETTER TO MY MOM

Kathleen Anderson

Dear Mom,

I wanted to do something special for you this Christmas, as I've done in previous years. My daily devotional calendar (which you gave me for my birthday) had these words on December 6, and they gave me an idea:

"God gave us memories that we might have roses in December," by Sir James M. Barrie.

Seeing the word *memories* was all I needed. My mind immediately went racing back to past Christmases, and all the happy memories I have of them came flooding over me. That's when I decided I would write down some of them for you to read, and hopefully it will make you happy to know that you and Dad left so many good ones with Eileen, Jim, and me. Some of them are such silly little things, and I find it interesting that I'm reminded of them. But then, little things *do* mean a lot.

One of the greatest memories, of course, was going to get the Christmas tree from the Hoovers' farm with the tractor and trailer—especially after it had snowed. Most of his trees were quite large, and Dad usually had to cut them down to size. I can realize now that that was not an easy thing to do, especially when he let me "help him" saw it. And I remember that frequently the trees didn't look quite the same on the ground as they did when standing high above us in the grove. Those are the times when Dad would stand outside the back porch door at the bottom of the steps and try to wire and/or nail extra tree branches in place (while following our instructions to "Move it up" or "Move it left" or "Make sure it's not upside down!") so it would be *the perfect tree*, something that was always so important to me, for whatever reason.

However, in looking back at some of the pictures and seeing how I overloaded most of the trees with tinsel, I'm amazed that you *allowed* me to decorate them! It was so special to me then, though, and I thought they looked so beautiful. And you and Dad always made me feel that you also thought the trees looked beautiful. I thank you both for that. Sparing my feelings was much more important than having a tree everyone would rave about, and you understood that.

I can remember unpacking the Christmas ornaments each year and looking at them with wonder. And seeing them today as an adult still brings to mind comforting memories and the wonder of those Christmases long ago. Even the angel from the top of our tree, still looking beautiful despite her many years of warming our home with her glow, continues to warm my heart and translate me back to a time of wonderful memories.

That's not to say that the true meaning of Christmas wasn't always emphasized in our home, because it was. The Christmas story was read, as was book after book of other Christmas stories. And I remember that the nativity scene (usually on the buffet or the mantel) was always the first thing to be put up. And, naturally, it was always arranged over and over again before the big day.

Being in Christmas programs was another highlight. Our city choir director always worked wonders with us, and I was so filled with the beauty of the season that on many a night when we sang in the candlelit church with hundreds of singers from churches all over the city, the words would barely come out of my throat, because it was almost always choked with emotion.

I even relish the memory of one of my more enthusiastic endeavors. I was trying to reproduce a picture from a magazine that showed marshmallow people gliding effortlessly across a mirror of ice. For some reason, my hills made of cotton, my ice mirror, and my marshmallow skaters never materialized. As the cotton hills sagged and caved in, my candy-cane trees fell over, and the marshmallow people kept falling apart on the ice, I decided to give up. But instead of making me feel like a failure, you and Dad suggested that we make hot chocolate and put the marshmallows on top. Then we sat in front of the fire and drank it, and suddenly the situation didn't seem so awful after all.

I was never one for dolls (that was Eileen's department), and my closest concession to them, as I recall, was the Storybook dolls, which I stood on the mantel from end to end for several years. Little did any of us know that they were probably the forerunners of the Barbie doll and would be worth a fortune if we'd kept them! Why didn't I? I certainly kept everything else.

The year Dad got you a pale green hassock (usually referred to today as an ottoman) was very exciting as it was the BIGGEST present anyone had ever gotten for Christmas. He made us promise not to tell, and that was a big part of all the excitement—watching him hide it while you weren't at home. I can remember all the tricks we used to try to keep you from going upstairs so you wouldn't see the big box on your way down and begin to speculate about what was in it. We wanted it to be a surprise as much as Dad did. You enjoyed it so much, as that was in the days before recliners, and of course Dad was so pleased. I think all of us kids were more excited watching you open your big gift that year than we were about opening ours.

One of my BEST Christmases was the year that most of my presents were books. I actually got out a yardstick and measured the height of the stack when I piled them all up. *Wildfire* was one of them, I recall. All the reading to us you and Dad did really paid off! It's still something all three of us kids enjoy immensely and something which has certainly been passed on.

Another great Christmas was the year I got the record *Sixteen Tons*, by Tennessee Ernie Ford, on Christmas Eve—before I had even received the record player! I was so excited that night I could hardly sleep because that was to be my biggest surprise ever for Christmas! That was one time knowing ahead of time what I was getting didn't matter at all. Although there were a few times when I did peek, I soon realized on Christmas morning that I'd only spoiled it for myself so I did that very few times!

The Christmas Eves we spent at our house on Amherst Road are also as vivid in my mind today as if they had just happened yesterday. It was so exciting waiting at the front window to see who would arrive first—Grandma and Grandpa McKelvey, the McPeeks, or the Burgers. Helping them carry in the presents was always fun because, if I really got lucky, I'd see some of mine and get a chance to squeeze and shake them.

Then everyone would help load the groaning table with all the food that everyone had prepared, and we'd all gather around it to thank God for sending us His Son as our greatest gift. After eating and cleaning up the kitchen immediately (a McKelvey curse I have inherited!), one of my best memories is of sitting beside Dad on the piano bench, turning the pages for him as we sang Christmas carols around the piano. That always made me feel so important. And he always told me that I turned the pages at exactly the right time.

Even after Dad died, you did everything you could to make Christmases the same for us so it wouldn't be so hard. I'll never forget how especially painful the first Christmas without Dad was, but I now look back in total admiration at all you did to help us through it.

And in looking back, the one thing I always remember feeling when I went to bed on Christmas Eve, and every other night, was a sense of security that came from knowing the strength of the love that you and Dad had for each other and for us children. That feeling has never changed. It has been a constant in my life, and one I wouldn't trade for anything.

I know I've said it before, but it bears repeating. Of all the parents I've ever known, I truly would not have traded mine for anything. As time goes on, I realize more and more just how precious the time spent with family really is. You were making wonderful memories for us back then when we were children, and you probably weren't even aware of it. And it's now our responsibility to carry on with that tradition by making happy memories for our families.

Thank you so much for making Christmas such a time of wonder for all of us.

With all my love,

Kath[9]

A WONDROUS WORD

Old German Carol

Words by Elsie Duncan Yale

As midnight hush so calm and still
Was brooding o'er the vale and hill,
The shepherds 'neath the starry light
Were watching o'er their flocks by night.
But a wondrous word,
Thro' the silence heard,
It was "Glory be to God, to God on high!"

Bright starbeams crown'd the dreaming plain,
The night wind breath'd a soft refrain,
O'er David's town dark shadows crept,
As shepherds still their vigil kept.
But a wondrous word,
Thro' the silence heard,
It was "Glory be to God, to God on high!"

O holy night, O night divine!
What tender joy, what peace is thine!
For 'mid thy silence seraphs come
To herald one from heav'nly home.
But a wondrous word,
Thro' the silence heard,
It was "Glory be to God, to God on high!"

Glory to God, be God on high,
Peace unto earth, unto earth is nigh;
Glory to God, list the reply!
It is glory to God, unto God on high.

A mother never forgets the first time she sees her child. She memorizes in her heart the wonder of each tiny feature. She runs her fingertip tenderly across her infant's silken skin. She checks each finger and toe. Her heart skips a beat as tiny eyes look up at her—helpless except for her protection and care. Mary must have felt the same wonder as she gazed down at her sweet baby boy, lying in His manger bed. Jesus was indeed the Savior of the world, but for those first precious moments, He was simply Mary's Child.

Rebecca Currington

To travel the road
to Bethlehem

is to keep a rendezvous
with *wonder,*

to answer the
call of *wisdom,*

and to bow the knee
in *worship.*

John A. Knight

Christmas Is
HOPE

We rejoice in the

hope of the glory of God.

Romans 5:2 NIV

CHRISTMAS IS HOPE

Hope is the very essence of the life of God. Without it we would perish in darkness and despair, unable to reach out for and receive the gift of eternal life. When that sweet baby was born and placed in Bethlehem's manger, our hope was born with Him. As He grew in wisdom and stature, our hope grew with Him. As He walked through the countryside healing the sick and restoring sight to the blind, our hope increased with every miraculous touch of His healing hands. When He gave His life on Calvary's Cross, our hope was purchased, and when He rose from the grave, our hope was forever secured.

Shouldn't it be our mission to shine the light of hope into every heart we encounter? In each basket of Christmas goodies, each note written within a Christmas card, each gift carefully chosen and meticulously wrapped, every act of kindness and goodwill, you deliver hope to the world. You are an ambassador of hope, and when better to carry out your mission than at Christmas?

What is Christmas?

It is *tenderness* for the past,
courage for the present,
hope for the future.

It is a fervent wish that

every cup may overflow

with blessings rich and eternal,

and that *every path*

may lead to

peace.

Agnes M. Pahro

Rise, happy morn, rise, holy morn,

Draw forth the cheerful day from night;

O Father, touch the east, and light

The light that shone when *Hope was born.*

Alfred Lord Tennyson

Advent is concerned with the connection between

memory and hope, which is so necessary to man.

Advent's intention is to awaken the

most profound and basic emotional memory within us,

namely, the memory of *the God who became a child.*

This is a healing memory;

it brings hope.

Pope Benedict XVI

I have set the LORD always before me;

Because *He is* at my right hand

I shall not be moved.

Therefore my heart is glad,

and my glory rejoices;

My flesh also will rest in hope.

PSALM 16:8–9 NKJV

COME THOU LONG-EXPECTED JESUS

Charles Wesley

Come, Thou long-expected Jesus,
Born to set Thy people free;
From our fears and sins release us;
Let us find our rest in Thee.
Israel's strength and consolation
Hope of all the earth Thou art;
Dear desire of every nation,
Joy of every longing heart.

Born Thy people to deliver,
Born a Child and yet a King,
Born to reign in us for ever,
Now Thy gracious kingdom bring.
By Thine own eternal Spirit
Rule in all our hearts alone;
By Thine own sufficient merit,
Raise us to Thy glorious throne.

CHRISTMAS FRUIT COOKIES

Leave these on the table for Santa. He'll love you for it!

Ingredients:

1 pound dates, pitted

3 slices candied pineapple

6 cups pecans

1 tsp. vanilla extract

1 cup sugar

4 eggs

1½ cups all-purpose flour

2 tsp. baking powder

Pinch of salt

½ pound green and red
candied cherries

Instructions:

Chop dates, pineapple, and pecans together. Add vanilla, and let mixture sit overnight in a covered bowl in the refrigerator. Add the remaining ingredients, mix well, and drop by spoonfuls onto a greased and floured cookie sheet. Bake 10 minutes at 300°F. Remove from the oven and add a cherry to each one. Cook 5 additional minutes. Store in a tightly sealed can.

Christmas takes us *back to hope*

brought forth in swaddling cloths

in a manger;

it looks *forward to the hope*

of the cross.

Cassandra M. Harrington

BENARD'S STORY

Deena C. Bouknight

A few Christmases ago, a simple, clear plastic box filled with dollar-store purchases was placed into the hands of a twelve-year-old Ugandan boy named Benard. When he opened the box, he found much-needed items like socks, a toothbrush, and soap, as well as paper, pencils, pens, and a ruler. On the bottom of the box, he found a letter from my eight-year-old son, Justin. Those simple gifts, specially selected by Justin and sent from our home in Columbia, South Carolina, planted a seed of hope in Benard's heart. This is how he responded.

> Greetings to you,
>
> I thank you very much for the Christmas gifts you sent me. It is very good, and I feel very happy with it. I thank God very much to have a friend like you who cares for needy children like me. May God bless you so much.
>
> Yours friendly,
>
> Benard

Orphaned and residing in the Kampala health department, where his uncle served as a night watchman, it was Benard's best Christmas in a long time. The Christmases that were to come would grow the rooted seed into a vine bearing much fruit not only for Benard but also for our family on the opposite side of the globe. Benard's next letter expressed a need felt by children worldwide:

> *I am very glad to have a golden chance to write my letter to you. How are you? On my side, I am fine and my uncle too. I would like to inform you that since the new year begun, I haven't gone to school because of no school fees since my parents are not there.*
>
> *Yours faithfully,*
>
> *Benard*

Approximately 115 million primary school–age children in the world do not have access to the money necessary to pay school fees and purchase books and supplies. School fees can consume nearly a quarter of a poor person's income. In Uganda, like in other parts of the world, it is estimated that one in five children are unable to attend school. Living in a culture where education has always been free, it first appalled and then saddened me. It caused Justin and his younger sister to sit up and take notice. It gave them a new appreciation for something they had always taken for granted. Yet, after checking with various relief organizations and pleading for assistance, we received this discouraging response: "Do you know how many children want to attend school and can't?" was the general answer. "Pray about it and decide what *you* want to do."

Prayer prompted me to check into the cost of school fees for a term at Aliba Primary School—the place from which Benard's letter had been posted. I learned that the fees amounted to thirty dollars in U.S. currency. Thirty dollars. About the price of one pizza dinner for a family of four.

We wired the money to the school and unexpectedly received an e-mail from the director of the health department. He thanked us for giving a poor orphan boy in his country some hope. Eventually, Benard was allowed to e-mail us as well. The messages were simple and fragmented, but they expressed his heart:

> *Hello, how are u doing? I think all of us are fine. I got English 46, math 54, science 58, social studies 62. The total mark was 220. I want to thank you very much for giving me a great support last term. May almighty God reward and give strength to save God's people. Amen. Today at the church, they preached to us from the book according to Isaiah 55:6–13 and the second reading was from the gospel of Matthew 6:33–35. I enjoyed today's services real much.*
>
> *May God bless u all. AMEN.*
>
> *Benard*

For the next Christmas, Benard received much more than just a small plastic box. A large shipment of books, including a new Bible, some illustrated classics, and a simple prayer book was sent to him. His e-mailed response expressed unparalleled joy and awe at the opportunity to "own" books, a delight reserved only for the wealthy in his country.

We began to learn about Benard's interest in soccer, about his friends, about his tribal village, and about the languages and customs of Uganda. When we celebrated the Fourth of July, we asked him about his own flag. When we planted herbs and tomatoes in the summer, we learned of the importance of his self-sustaining maize garden.

Then one day we received a frantic message from Benard. It came to light that his uncle struggled with alcohol. He had flown into a violent rage and driven Benard from their residence. In his e-mail, Benard said that he feared for his life on the streets of Kampala. He asked us, whom he now referred to as his "Mommy Deena" and his "lovely family," to pray for him.

We *did* pray and God intervened!

By way of a divine coincidence, a friend of ours happened to be in Uganda at the time, installing water systems around Lake Victoria. An e-mail was sent to him about Benard's situation, and he telephoned the school where Benard attended. Miraculously, our friend was able to speak to him and assure him of God's protective hand. Soon after, an e-mail arrived from Benard saying that he and his uncle had reconciled.

Just a few months later, however, Benard sent word that his uncle had passed away. He asked us again to pray for him and to offer any suggestions about where he should live and what he should do. The awareness of the great distance between Uganda and America suddenly became very real to us—especially to me. My mother's heart yearned to purchase a $2,000 plane ticket, find the dark, lanky boy, and comfort him with an embrace. Realistically, though, my options were seriously limited. After much prayer, I urged Benard to seek help from the church he had been attending. "Tell your fellow believers about your situation," I counseled. "I believe they will help you." What soon followed was this e-mail:

> How are u all. I am fine. I now stay with a family in Kampala. They are strong Christians right from their grand parents. They are lovely family. Always when ever we go to bed we must pray.
>
> Take care,
>
> Benard

Once again, we rejoiced. God had provided a safe place for Benard among Christians. I have since learned that even though the need is great for many, Ugandans have a strong sense of family and will do whatever they can to care for those in need.

We continue to remain close to Benard, even though we are separated by such a wide expanse. We have prayed for and encouraged Benard through malaria, hookworms, and fear. We have provided him with money for a mosquito net and eyeglasses. And, for each Christmas, we have sent, along with much love, gifts that we felt would brighten his days and help him grow in his walk with God.

> *I thank u very much to tell me about the Frisbee because I thought that it was a plate for eating food and I had kept it in my school bag in order to save my lunch at school.*
>
> *Yours lovely,*
>
> *Benard*

Benard's future is more hopeful because of our connection with him, yet it is our lives that are forever changed. It is our prayer, especially Mommy Deena's, that we will be able to visit the country we have learned so much about because of a boy. Perhaps we will even be able to meet the precious boy who opened that simple plastic box. It is my prayer that I will one day embrace him. Christmas has become a much sweeter and more meaningful celebration. Benard has opened to us a brand-new world of sharing and blessing.

> *Praise the living God. I thank almighty God for giving me this great chance among other children. It is real God's love which unites us as one family of God to be together.*
>
> *God be with u and all your family.*
>
> *Benard*[10]

There's more, much more to Christmas

Than candle-light and cheer;

It's the spirit of sweet friendship,

That brightens all the year;

It's thoughtfulness and kindness,

It's hope reborn again,

For peace, for understanding

And for goodwill to men!

Author Unknown

When compassion for the common man was born on Christmas Day, with it was born new hope among the multitudes. They feel a great, ever-rising determination to lift themselves and their children out of hunger and disease and misery, up to a higher level. Jesus started a fire upon the earth, and it is burning hot today, the fire of a new hope in the hearts of the hungry multitudes.

Frank C. Laubach

God must have been filled with hope and anticipation that day, that special day. It was the day His plan to redeem the human race finally began to unfold. The preparations had all been made. He had chosen the place, a lowly stable in Bethlehem. And He had chosen the mother, a young virgin with a pure heart. God the Father and God the Son had been together for eternity—but Jesus agreed to the plan. He would be the Redeemer, born into a human body in order to redeem regrettable choices.

God knew when He endowed His creation with free will that He would be unable to control the choices made. Still He longed to be loved for Himself, so He gave each man, woman, and child the privilege to choose. When those choices went awry, His heart was broken, but He wasn't defeated. He had a plan in mind. That must have been a good day for Him, a special day, the day His plan unfolded. It must have been a day when hope was born anew in His heart.

Andrea Garney

Christmas Is
MEMORIES

This I recall to my mind,

therefore have I hope.

LAMENTATIONS 3:21 KJV

CHRISTMAS IS MEMORIES

Christmastime for most of us is like a break in the clouds that lets the sunshine in. Eleven months of the year, we execute our busy schedules, deal with the exigencies of our lives, and bury our sorrows deep down inside. But there's something about Christmas, something that allows us to set work aside for family, hope for a new beginning and a better tomorrow, and open ourselves to others. Perhaps that's why we so treasure our Christmases. Somehow God uses them to recast even the difficult and painful episodes of our lives in a more pleasing hue.

So celebrate your Christmas memories this year. Get out the pictures and pass them around. Live, love, and laugh. Let your heart be light. For a while, let down your defenses and settle into the moment. And while you're at it, don't forget to take as many photos as you can. This year like all the others will one day be a memory you will cherish.

It comes every year and
will go on forever. And
along with Christmas belong

the *keepsakes and the customs.*
Those humble, everyday
things a mother clings to,
and ponders,
like Mary in the

secret spaces
of her heart.

Marjorie Holmes

My first copies of *Treasure Island* and

Huckleberry Finn still have

some blue-spruce needles scattered

in the pages. *They smell of*

Christmas still.

Charlton Heston

WELCOME CHRISTMAS

Sonja Jacobsen

It's time to welcome Christmas
To our home again this year.
All the gifts and joyous singing;
All the greetings of good cheer;
All the stockings on the mantle hang;
All the candles burning bright;
All the snowflakes on the window pane;
All the dreams we dream tonight.

Yes, it's time to welcome Christmas
As we have in years gone by.
All our gifts tied up with ribbons,
All the smells of Christmas pie.
All the ivy, cones, and holly;
All the angels on the tree;
All the old folks feeling jolly;
That's all Christmas Eve should be.[11]

HOLIDAY HASH BROWN CASSEROLE

Serve it to your family on Christmas morning
and make a memory.

Ingredients:

1 package (12 ounces) frozen
hash-brown potatoes

¼ cup (½ stick) melted
salted butter

1 cup diced bacon

8 ounces shredded cheese
of your choice

½ can (10 ounces) Ro*Tel
Mexican Lime and Cilantro

2 eggs

½ cup milk

¼ tsp. salt

Instructions:

Preheat the oven to 425°F. Grease 10-inch pie pan with butter.
Put the hash browns into the pan and brush them with remaining
melted butter. Bake for 25 minutes. Remove from oven and layer
bacon, cheese, and Ro*Tel over the top. Combine eggs, milk, and
salt, and pour over the top. Bake 30–35 minutes at 350°F.

Christmas is a day of
meaning and traditions,
a special day spent in
the *warm circle of*
family and friends.

Margaret Thatcher

Happy, happy Christmas, that can win us back to the delusions of our childish days; that can recall to the old man the *pleasures of his youth;* that can transport the sailor and the traveller, thousands of miles away, *back to his own fire-side and his quiet home!*

Charles Dickens

Like snowflakes,
my *Christmas memories*
gather and dance—each
beautiful, unique,
and too soon gone.

Deborah Whipp

A NIGHT WRAPPED IN SONG

Lydia E. Harris

The chilly wind blew as I huddled with other carolers outside our country church. I drew in the cold, crisp night air, shivering with excitement. After years of waiting, my turn had come. I was finally old enough to carol all night with the church choir. With church folk scattered throughout the rural area around Blaine, Washington, it would take most of the night to carol at each member's doorstep. Bundled in my green woolen scarf and new gloves, I couldn't wait to begin.

I remembered past Christmas Eves when I had watched my seven older brothers and sisters leave the warmth of our family gathering at 11 P.M. to carol. How I had longed to go with them. At bedtime, I would beg my mother, "Please, wake me when the carolers come." She always tried, but sometimes she couldn't rouse me.

As I grew older, my mother found it easier to awaken me in the middle of the night. Sleepy-eyed and pajama-clad, I would peek out the dormer window of our large green-and-white farmhouse. I would listen dreamily to the carolers with my nose pressed against the frosty window. They sounded like angels, singing "Joy to the World" and "Silent Night." I returned their cheerful shouts of "Merry Christmas!"

and nestled back in bed, wishing I could join in the fun.

Now, after years of yearning and waiting, my turn had come at last. The wind nipped my rosy cheeks. *A few snowflakes would make it perfect,* I thought. The choir director's voice interrupted my dreaming.

"Let's get organized," he said. "How many of you can take your cars?" I looked around at the young men offering to drive. I hoped to sit in the front seat between a couple of them. But other teenage girls experienced at flirting won those seats. I piled into the backseat with friends, just excited to be going along.

We laughed and chatted as we drove through the countryside, stopping to sing for church members. By starlight and flashlight, we crunch, crunch, crunched our way over the frozen ground to the front doors of farmers' homes. Most folks expected us and flung their doors wide open, inviting us in for a snack, even at two or three in the morning. Sipping hot chocolate by the crackling fires warmed us inside and out. Their generous hospitality forced the choir director to limit the number of families allowed to feed us. Otherwise, we'd get sick from feasting in each home. Even so, we waddled to the cars stuffed like fat Christmas geese.

We continued to the next homes, refueled with sloppy joes, hot dogs, and fudge. As the night wore on, our throats wore out from singing in the winter air. We sounded more like croaking frogs than the angelic choir I remembered hearing as a child.

Arriving home at five in the morning, I snuggled beneath my thick handmade quilt. I tried to snatch a few hours of sleep before the Christmas-morning church service where the choir would sing again. But it seemed hard to fall asleep with the excitement so fresh in my mind.

The night had been better than I had imagined. No, I didn't hear angelic hosts sing "Glory to God in the Highest" to country shepherds, but I sang of His birth to country church members. I didn't see one bright star in the sky, but I sang by starlight about that "star of wonder, star of night." I didn't bow at a manger to touch a newborn infant, but God touched me as I worshiped the newborn King when I sang, "O come, let us adore Him."

More than forty years later, all-night caroling on Christmas Eve remains a treasured memory. I savor those magical nights wrapped in song that warmed me like my new woolen scarf.

A few years ago, I returned to the Mennonite church of my childhood and asked the pianist, "Does the choir still carol all night on Christmas Eve?"

Her face broke into a wide grin. "We sure do!"

This Christmas Eve in northwestern Washington, carolers will again awaken sleepy-eyed children and serenade waiting families. They'll stuff themselves with homemade treats throughout the frosty night. And little ones will long to join the caroling choir and sing praises to the Christ Child under starlit skies.

It cheers my heart to know the caroling tradition lives beyond my dreams, creating treasured memories for another generation of youthful carolers.[12]

When we recall *Christmas past,*

we usually find that the *simplest things*—

not the great occasions—

give off the *greatest glow of happiness.*

Bob Hope

OLD-FASHIONED PEANUT BRITTLE

This is a crunchy, delicious Christmas delight.

Ingredients:

2½ cups granulated sugar

¼ cup (½ stick) unsalted butter

⅔ cup water

1½ cups lightly salted peanuts

Instructions:

Grease and line a 9 x 13-inch baking pan with waxed paper. Combine the sugar, butter, and water in a large saucepan. Stirring occasionally, cook until the mixture turns golden brown. Remove from heat and stir in the peanuts. Pour the mixture into the prepared pan and let it cool. Break into pieces. Place in an airtight container and decorate with ribbon.

SO REMEMBER

Author Unknown

So remember while December

Brings the only Christmas Day,

In the year let there be Christmas

In the things you do and say;

Wouldn't life be worth the living

Wouldn't dreams be coming true

If we kept the Christmas spirit

All the whole year through?

CHRISTMAS MEMORY ORNAMENTS

Christmas tree ornaments can be a wonderful way to document your children's growing-up years. Each year, select an ornament that represents an important activity or accomplishment for each child for that year. This might be a golf ball ornament for your son who is learning to play or an automobile ornament for your daughter who just learned to drive.

As you decorate the tree together, present the new ornaments for that year to be placed on the tree. After Christmas, have each child take down their ornaments, wrap them, and place them in the storage box. Before long, your family will have an ornamental history of each child's life.

BELLS ACROSS THE SNOW

Frances Ridley Havergal

O Christmas! merry Christmas!
Is it really come again,
With its memories and greetings,
With its joy and with its pain?
There's a minor in the carol,
And a shadow in the light,
And a spray of cypress twining
With the holly wreath tonight.
And the hush is never broken
By laughter light and low,
As we listen in the starlight
To the "bells across the snow."

CHRISTMAS TOYS FROM THE 1880s

- **Dollhouses** with elaborate furnishings. These included cabinetry, pianos, leather library sets, dining-room sets, lamps, gilded clocks, even busts mounted on pedestals.

- **Walking toys.** The most popular were a rooster that crowed as it walked, an elephant that moved slowly, an ape that clambered along awkwardly, and a pig that jumped out of a box.

- **Alphabet blocks.** These squares of differing sizes had letters painted on them.

- **Animal Penny Banks.** Children deposited their pennies into the open mouths of the animals and the money dropped into their ample bodies.

- **Tops.** Some worked by electricity and changed colors if touched while they were spinning.

- **Wooden animals.** For younger children, these were well-carved and without paint. For older children, there were leather-covered animals.

CHRISTMAS TOYS FROM THE 1980s

- **Transformers.** These robot action figures could be manipulated into the shapes of cars, trucks, airplanes, and various other vehicles.

- **My Little Pony.** Girls loved these little ponies that came in various colors with flowing manes and symbols painted on their bodies. They came with accessories and different hairstyles.

- **Teenage Mutant Ninja Turtles.** Raphael, Michelangelo, Leonardo, and Donatello were reptilian heroes and crime fighters. They spawned dozens of action figures and even a cartoon show and video games.

- **G.I. Joe.** Originally created as a cartoon character in 1942, this action figure became America's most popular soldier.

Time was, with most of us, when *Christmas Day* encircling all our limited world like a magic ring, left nothing out for us to miss or seek; bound together all our home enjoyments, affections, and hopes; grouped everything and everyone around the Christmas fire; and made the little picture shining in our bright young eyes, complete.

Charles Dickens

Christmas Is
GIVING

The Lord himself will give you a sign: The
virgin will be with child and will give birth
to a son, and will call him Immanuel.

ISAIAH 7:14 NIV

CHRISTMAS IS GIVING

God has given a gift so precious, so magnificent, so grand that we will always be in His debt. The wise men recognized the enormous worth of His gift, as did the shepherds. Mary and Joseph were amazed by His gift—so amazed that they could not help but praise Him. Even the priests in the temple grasped the incalculable nature of His gift and counted it a privilege to give their blessing.

God gave us Jesus, His only begotten Son—His gift was wrapped not in elegant foil but simple swaddling clothes, illuminated not by the lights of the tree but rather the lights of a brilliant star. God's gift was given thoughtfully, respectfully, and without reservation.

What can you say about your giving? Do you give of yourself, your time, and your possessions generously without expectation of return? Do you give from the heart rather than from obligation? Do the gifts you are able to give serve as reminders of God's goodness to you? Let each gift you give, whether great or small, prestigious or humble, costly or priceless, reflect the nature of the greatest Gift and the greatest Giver of all!

Let us remember that the Christmas heart is a giving heart, a wide-open heart that thinks of others first. The birth of the baby Jesus stands as the most significant event in all history, because it has meant the pouring into a sick world of the healing medicine of love which has transformed all manner of hearts for almost two thousand years. . . . Underneath all the bulging bundles is this beating Christmas heart.

George Matthew Adams

The magi, as you know,

were wise men—

wonderfully wise men—

who brought gifts to the Babe in the manger.

They invented the art of

giving Christmas presents.

O. Henry

Unless we make Christmas

an occasion to share our blessings,

all the snow in Alaska

won't make it "white."

Bing Crosby

Do give books—religious or otherwise—for Christmas.

They're never fattening,

seldom sinful,

and permanently personal.

Lenore Hershey

To give
out of the abundance
of a heart of love,
that is the *real spirit
of Christmas!*

The *best gift* around any *Christmas tree*

is the presence
of a *happy family*
all wrapped up
in each other.

Burton Hillis

HANDMADE CLAY ORNAMENTS

Help your little ones make these for their family and friends.

Ingredients:

1⅛ cup all-purpose flour

¾ cup ground cinnamon

1 cup salt

1 Tbsp. ground nutmeg

1 Tbsp. ground cloves

1 cup water

Instructions:

Combine the dry ingredients with the water. Stir until the mixture becomes a smooth, stiff dough. Divide into three or four portions and place each portion between two sheets of waxed paper. Roll out to about ¼ inch thick. Use cookie cutters to cut dough into the shapes of Christmas trees, stars, bells, candy canes, and other Christmas shapes. While the dough is still soft, use a straw to make a hole near the top of each ornament. Bake for 15–20 minutes at 350ºF. When cooled, insert a colorful ribbon through each hole and tie it into a bow so you can hang it on the tree.

CHRISTMAS GIFT SUGGESTIONS

To your enemy, *give forgiveness.*

To an opponent, *give tolerance.*

To a friend, *give your heart.*

To a customer, *give service.*

To all, *give charity.*

To every child, *give a good example.*

To yourself, *give respect.*

Oren Arnold

THE BEST CHRISTMAS PRESENT EVER

Nancy Julien Kopp

In 1949 the twenty-one children in my fifth-grade class learned one of life's greatest lessons. Ten-year-olds usually care more about the importance of receiving gifts than considering the joy in giving them. But that year, we found out that giving truly is better than receiving, and it was all because of a special teacher.

Lyle Biddinger served on a navy destroyer during World War II, went to college on the GI Bill, and landed in a Chicago suburban grade school teaching fifth grade. We were his first class, and he was the first male teacher in our kindergarten-through-eighth-grade school. Young, handsome, and an outstanding teacher—he was all any ten-year-old could ask for.

During family dinners, I talked endlessly about what Mr. Bid had told us that day, what he'd shown us, the games he'd taught us. He may as well have been sitting at our table every night, for his presence was evident Monday through Friday. I hurried through breakfast so I could get to school early, and I offered to stay after class and do whatever little jobs needed to be done. I wasn't the only one who acted this way about Mr. Biddinger—we all adored him.

We were so proud to be in his class that we preened our feathers like peacocks around the kids in the other fifth grade. He was all ours, and like kids of that age, we let everyone know it. Our teacher made learning fun, and in the 1940s this was a new approach. At one point, some of the parents went to the principal and complained that Mr. Biddinger spent too much time playing games during class time. School should not be fun; it was to be hard work. Somehow Mr. Biddinger and the principal placated the disgruntled parents, and life went on as before in the fifth grade.

December arrived, and the room mother contacted the other parents. Each family was asked to give a modest amount of money to be used for a Christmas gift for the teacher. It was not an unusual request in our school. Next she called Mr. Biddinger's wife to find out what might be the perfect gift for him.

It was to be a secret, of course. But we all knew about it, and whispers and notes flew back and forth. Our class Christmas party would be held the last day before the holiday break. We would have a grab-bag gift exchange, punch, cookies, and candy. We'd play some games, get out of schoolwork, and give Mr. Bid his gift.

The days seemed to pass very slowly, and our excitement grew steadily. We looked forward to our school Christmas much more than the one we'd each have at home. Finally, the big day dawned. Our room mother arrived with the punch, brightly decorated Christmas cookies, and hard candies. But we were all wondering—where was the big box with the present for Mr. Bid? We hadn't seen her bring it in. We wriggled in our desks and fretted. Whispers sailed around the room until Mr. Bid scolded us. "Settle down," he said, "or the party's over as of now." Quiet reigned.

Soon enough, the treats and grab-bag gifts were passed out. We munched on our sugar cookies and slurped the red punch. The classroom door opened, and a strange woman walked in. Mr. Biddinger looked surprised at first; then a big smile crossed his face. We were soon introduced to his wife. The room mother disappeared into the hall but was back in seconds holding a good-sized box wrapped in Christmas paper and tied with a wide red ribbon. The chatter in the room ceased immediately, and all eyes were riveted on that box.

The room mother cleared her throat, walked to our teacher and said, "Mr. Biddinger, this gift is from your students. They wanted to show their love and appreciation by giving you something special." As she handed him the box, the room tingled with an air of excitement.

Mr. Bid seemed excited, and that thrilled us. He untied the bow and handed the ribbon to his wife. Next came the wrapping, as we all leaned forward to see. He opened the box and lifted a hunting jacket from the folds of tissue paper. This had been his fondest wish for Christmas, Mrs. Biddinger had told the room mother. Whenever possible he loved to hunt on the weekends, but the special hunting gear was beyond a teacher's salary at that time.

For the first time, the man who taught us so much became mute, totally speechless. He turned the jacket over and over and looked at the special pockets on the inside and outside. Having taken a few minutes to compose himself, he said, "This is probably the finest gift I've ever received." He didn't say why, but we knew. It was a gift of love from his first class—twenty-one ten-year-olds who adored him.

I don't remember the gifts I received at home that Christmas, but I'll never forget the gift we gave Mr. Biddinger. It was the best Christmas present ever.[13]

Christmas is

doing a *little something extra*

for someone.

Charles Schulz

What can I give Him,

Poor as I am?

If I were a shepherd,

I would bring a lamb.

If I were a wise man,

I would do my part;

Yet what I can I give Him?

Give my heart.

Christina Rossetti

It is the personal
thoughtfulness,
the warm human awareness,
the reaching out of the self
to one's fellow man
that makes giving worthy of the
Christmas spirit.

Isabel Currier

Christmas is the gift from heaven

of *God's Son given for free;*

If Christmas isn't found in your heart,

you won't find it under the tree.

Charlotte Carpenter

Christmas is based on an exchange of gifts:

the gift of God to man—

his Son;

and *the gift of man to God—*

when we first give *ourselves to God*.

Vance Havner

SUGGESTIONS FOR HANDMADE GIFTS

❄ Baked goods

❄ Original poems, stories, and paintings

❄ Help with yard work and chores

❄ Homemade jams and jellies

❄ An original song or musical composition

❄ Knitted and crocheted pieces

❄ Canned or frozen fruits and vegetables

❄ Shelled pecans or walnuts

THE BEST GIFTS OF ALL

❋ A gesture of love for the unlovely

❋ An act of kindness for the less fortunate

❋ A word of compassion for an aching heart

❋ A sign of respect for the disenfranchised

❋ A prayer of hope for the hopeless

❋ A tender hug for the lonely

❋ A warm meal for the hungry

❋ A safe place to sleep for the homeless

❋ A word of witness for those who walk in darkness

HOLIDAY NUTS

This treat is elegant enough to wrap and place under the tree for your favorite people.

Ingredients:

2 cups pecan halves

2 cups walnut halves

½ cup water

1½ cups sugar

1 tsp. ground cinnamon

Instructions:

Spread nuts in a single layer in a 9 x 13-inch pan. Bake at 325°F for 20 minutes or until lightly toasted. Cool in pan on a rack. Place the water and sugar in a heavy saucepan and bring to a boil. Simmer uncovered until it reaches the soft-ball stage. Remove from heat and stir in cinnamon. Add the toasted nuts and coat well. Pour onto waxed paper and separate. Cool. Store in an airtight container in a cool place.

'Tis the season for

kindling the *fire of hospitality*

in the hall, . . .

the genial *flame of charity*

in the heart.

Washington Irving

GIFT GIVERS AROUND THE WORLD

America—Santa Claus

England—Father Christmas

France—Père Noël

Germany—Christkind (an angelic messenger from Jesus)

Holland—Saint Nicholas

Spain and South America—The Three Kings

Russia—Babouschka (a grandmotherly figure) and Grandfather Frost

In an effort to give her ten-year-old daughter something practical for Christmas, a woman suggested opening a savings account for her. Her daughter was delighted. Mother and daughter went to the bank. "Since it's your account," the mother said, "you should fill out the application." This went just fine until the daughter came to the space:

Name of your former bank.

After a slight hesitation, she wrote: *Piggy*.

Author Unknown

Christmas is a gift from God.

He gave *His light* to pierce the darkness of our souls,

His love to thaw the coldness of our hearts,

His truth to break the chains of our bondage,

His peace to quiet the voices of our guilt,

His Son to pay the price for our eternal salvation.

D. Valentine

You can never truly enjoy Christmas

until you can look up

into the Father's face and tell

him you have *received*

his Christmas gift.

John Richard Rice

Gifts of time and love
are surely the basic ingredients of
a truly merry Christmas.

Peg Bracken

Christmas Is
for
CHILDREN

Jesus said to them, "Let the little children

come to me, and do not hinder them, for the

kingdom of God belongs to such as these."

MARK 10:14 NIV

CHRISTMAS IS FOR CHILDREN

Christmas, like faith, is best viewed through the eyes of a child. Somehow our adult minds rule out too many possibilities, impose too many limitations, require too many explanations. At Christmastime, though, we allow ourselves to be swept up in demonstrations of love and expressions of joy. We give without hesitation, smile at strangers, submerge ourselves in an ocean of excitement and expectation. In other words, we become like children—if but for the season.

God endorses this childlike behavior. He even says it is the norm in the Kingdom of God. So observe the children in your life and learn from them how to wrap your arms around the wonders of this special time of year. Then use what you learn in your celebrations to become a more loving, more giving, more joyous, more peaceful, more hopeful, more faith-filled person all year long.

UNDER THE BOUGH

Samuel Taylor Coleridge

On the evening before Christmas Day, one of the parlors is lighted up by the children, into which the parents must not go. A great yew bough is fastened on the table at a little distance from the wall, a multitude of little tapers are fastened in the bough, but not so as to burn it, till they are nearly burnt out, and colored paper, etc., hangs and flutters from the twigs. Under this bough the children lay out in great neatness the presents they mean for their parents, still concealing

in their pockets what they intend for each other. Then the parents are introduced, and each presents his little gift—and then they bring out the others, and present them to each other with kisses and embraces. . . . I was very much affected, and the shadow of the bough on the wall, and arching over on the ceiling, made a pretty picture.

THE SPIRIT OF CHRISTMAS

Randy Richardson

As I read about creatures, some tall and some small,
who celebrate Christmas with no presents at all,
A lad, who had listened for twenty minutes now,
turned to his dad with a furrowed brow.
"Dad," the lad said, and then paused for a few,
indulging a thought as it grew and it grew.

Then that thought-filled bubble popped smack-dab in Dad's lap,
Just as he was considering a brief winter's nap.
How could a question so simple and sweet,
come from a lad of not even four feet?
"What's the spirit of Christmas?" he wanted to know.
He wanted to know, and he wouldn't let go.

Well, Dad, at first, squirmed just a bit,
Struggling to find an answer to fit.
Then it came to him, after a second or two,
Oh, this, he grinned, will most certainly do.
"It's a feeling," he said, "that comes from inside,"
and his chest began swelling just a little with pride.
But the boy wasn't done—no, no, not just yet.
There was still something he didn't quite get.

"Is it singing?" the child asked, looking like he would pop,
While Dad just wished that the questions would stop, stop, stop,
STOP!
"No, it's not, not exactly," Dad said with a wink.
But explaining isn't as easy as you think.
The spirit of Christmas is more than tinsel and toys.
But how do you impress that on little girls and boys?

He thought, and he thought, and he thought some more,
Until his head was feeling a little bit sore.
The question, that QUESTION, would not go away.
He searched for the words—the right ones to say.
Then, it came to him, the answer, that is, right there in his head,
But, by then, the lad was fast asleep in his bed.

So Dad tucked the boy in for the night,
Leaned over, kissed his cheek, and turned off the light.
The lad didn't need his answer right then,
He'd figure it out—just a matter of when.
Maybe it won't be until he's in his teens,
But one day he'll understand what it all means.

We, the grown-ups who pass down these holiday tales
must know that Christmas is more than cash-register sales.
Our wish lists should be inconsequential and small,
because Christmas isn't about us at all.
We should always give generously, as much as we can,
When we pass that bell-ringer, put a gift in the pan.
By example our children learn what it all means—
the gifts, the Giver, and the stuff in between.[14]

GUMDROP FLOAT

Gather the family and see who can make the prettiest float.

Ingredients:

2 scoops vanilla ice cream

1 can root beer

3 cherries

4 red and green gumdrops

Whipped cream topping

Instructions:

Scoop the ice cream into a tall glass. Slowly pour the root beer over the top. After the foam has settled, add whipped cream, cherries, and gumdrops.

What star is this, with beams so bright,

Which shame the sun's less radiant light?

'Tis sent to announce a newborn King,—

Glad tidings of our God to bring.

Translated from Latin by Rev. John Chandler

A CHILD'S SONG OF CHRISTMAS

Marjorie Lowry Christie Pickthall

My counterpane is soft as silk,
My blankets white as creamy milk.
The hay was soft to Him, I know,
Our little Lord of long ago.

Above the roof the pigeons fly
In silver wheels across the sky.
The stable-doves they cooed to them,
Mary and Christ in Bethlehem.

Bright shines the sun across the drifts,
And bright upon my Christmas gifts.
They brought Him incense, myrrh, and gold,
Our little Lord who lived of old.

O, soft and clear our mother sings
Of Christmas joys and Christmas things.
God's holy angels sang to them,
Mary and Christ in Bethlehem.

Our hearts they hold all Christmas dear,
And earth seems sweet and heaven seems near.
O, heaven was in His sight, I know,
That little Child of long ago.

THE SNOW GLOBE

Marie Norton

I sure wish it would snow," I said to my mom for the tenth time within just a few minutes. Snow was pretty unlikely in our small town south of Atlanta, Georgia. It only snowed once in a blue moon, and then it was just a dusting. My mother, Rose, wiped her hands on her apron after wiping a stray curl away from her face, leaving a flour smudge on her forehead. She was busy baking for the upcoming holidays—some cookies for me and a cake for the Harrisons who had just had a baby. She looked at me with understanding in her eyes, saying, "I know, honey, it would be nice, wouldn't it?" Then she gently pulled me to her side and gave me a hug with those flour-smudged hands.

It was the early 60s, and money was tight. My dad had hurt his back doing construction and was presently recuperating in bed. The doctor said it could be months before he was able to walk again, much less work. Mom was forced to find some means to bring in money. Not having much of an education limited her opportunities, so she ended up doing housework for a family in what I called the "rich" part of town. Every weekday Mom got me off to school and then rode the bus to Rosewood Estates, a very nice neighborhood with manicured green lawns and stately houses. Then after a hard day's work, she rode that bus home again and proceeded to cook supper and help me with homework and spend some time reading to my dad. And here it was Saturday, and she was baking for neighbors with a new baby and trying to bring some cheer to our own home with home-baked goodies for the upcoming holidays. She was amazing—I probably didn't appreciate that fact as much as I do now that I'm older and have children of my own. Even with all her troubles, she was always thinking of how she could make things special for others and especially for me, her only child.

Christmas was destined to be a humble affair that year so Mom told me she would make two new dresses for my dolly, Kate, out of some old scraps of fabric. She even let me choose the *good* fabric reserved for my church dresses. In addition, as a special gift, she promised to take me to the ice skating rink one evening—not to skate, because we couldn't afford that luxury, but I could watch and dream that I was on the ice and I was a famous world-class skater. I couldn't wait!

All of these things tumbled around in my head as I sat in class the next day, making it hard to concentrate on Mrs. Boswell's mathematical tables on the chalkboard. I daydreamed of waking up on Christmas morning with a foot of snow outside and a tree inside adorned with radiant jewels and merrily wrapped presents underneath. I had always been fascinated by snow—the pure white fluffy stuff that crumbles in your hands and sparkles so. Mom said ever since the time we visited an uncle in northern

Georgia and saw a real snowstorm, I had been mesmerized and talked of nothing else when Christmas would roll around. The pure whiteness of the trees and the countryside stuck with me—it reminded me of when my Sunday school teacher taught us about Jesus washing away our sins and making them like snow. And in the hard times we were going through, it also reminded me that a God who cares enough to wash away our sins and make us pure would also take care of us this Christmas. Right there at my desk, I breathed a prayer to God, *Help us, Lord, get back on our feet. And make this a special Christmas for all of us. Amen!*

Little did I know just how special that Christmas would be for us! The weeks leading up to Christmas Day seemed to be a blur—more baking, practicing for the Christmas play at church, finishing school reports before the holidays, keeping Dad company until Mom got home from work, and of course visiting the skating rink with Mom to watch the happy, bundled up people frolic on the ice. And finally, Christmas Eve came. I was overjoyed. Mom and Dad and I ate bread pudding in front of the fire and then Dad read the Christmas story before shooing me off to bed. I dreamt of snow, snow, and more snow.

The next morning, I awakened to loud knocking—who could that be on Christmas Day making all that racket on our front porch? I hurriedly put on my robe and scurried into the living room. There stood several people from our church—Mr. and Mrs. Hanson, Pastor Shepherd, and some ladies from the Missionary Society—all carrying paper bags filled with the biggest turkey I ever saw, several loaves of fresh-baked bread, some fruit and candy and a bolt of the most beautiful fabric I had ever seen. My parents were acting as dumbstruck as I felt. Then the pastor handed my dad an envelope, saying, "Tom, we know things have been tough for you and your family since your accident. We wanted to help. Merry Christmas!" My dad wiped the tears from his eyes and shook the pastor's hand warmly, saying, "Thank you so much. We are so grateful." Everyone then proceeded to unload all the gifts, and we all had a piece of Fanny Mae's famous chocolate cake, which she had baked just for us. Our guests were about to depart when Mrs. Hanson pulled out a small brightly wrapped box and placed it in my hands, saying, "Marie, the Lord told me to get this for you. I hope you like it." And then they were off before I even had time to unwrap it. After we said our good-byes, I rushed back inside to open my gift. I quickly tore off the wrapping paper and opened the box and found a beautiful snow globe. Inside the globe was a small country church sitting on a hillside dotted with trees. The trees were frosted with glitter, and the church sparkled like it was lit up from the inside. I gently turned it over, and all the snow fell upon the church and the trees. I immediately remembered my prayer to the Lord weeks before asking Him for help. He had heard my prayer. He had moved upon His people to help us, and He had even sent me a special gift to show His love. I was overwhelmed as I thanked Him again and again in my heart.

Even though that Christmas was many years ago, I still remember God's answer to my prayer. The money the church gave us that day helped us make it until my dad was able to work again. My mom was able to stay at home once more and take care of me and assist others in need. The snow globe that spoke so loudly of God's care still sits on my mantel today—a reminder of God's faithfulness and love. And today when I look out my window at Christmastime, I get to see, not dream of snow because I married a man from the hills of Tennessee.[15]

There's nothing sadder
in this world than to
awake Christmas morning and
not be a child.

Erma Bombeck

A legend tells that when Jesus was born

the *sun danced in the sky,*

the aged *trees straightened themselves*

and put on leaves and

sent forth the fragrance of blossoms once more.

These are the symbols of what

takes place in our hearts when the

Christ-Child is born anew each year.

Helen Keller

THE ALPHABET OF CHRISTMAS

Francis Jean Bechtel

A   is for the *animals* that lowed in the stable.

B   is for the *Baby Boy* with hay in His cradle.

C   is for *Christmas* when we celebrate His birth.

D   is for *destiny* that brought Him to Earth.

E   is for *epiphany*, for the wise men who came.

F   is for the *family* who gave Him His name.

G   is for *good will* and peace from above.

H   is for *hope* that we have through His love.

I   is for the *incarnation*, God lives among men.

J   is for *Jesus*, who took away sin.

K   is for *kings*, who came from afar.

L   is for the *light* of a very bright star.

M is for the *message* the Child came to bring.

N is for the *noels* we all love to sing.

O is for the *oxen*, who stood nearby.

P is for the *praise* from the angels on high.

Q is for the *questions* He answered for us.

R is for *redemption* when His name we trust.

S is for the *shepherds* who traveled to see.

T is for the *toys* under the tree.

U is for *unity*—to God we're brought near.

V is for *vision* that now is made clear.

W is for *wonderful counselor*, who showed us the way.

X is for *Xmas* (as the Greeks like to say).

Y is for the *yule log* that glows in the fire.

Z is for *Zion*, our true heart's desire.

CANDY CANE CAKE

This one is all about the children!

Ingredients:

⅔ cup unsalted butter

1⅔ cups sugar

3 eggs

½ tsp. vanilla extract

2 cups all-purpose flour

⅔ cup cocoa

1¼ tsp. baking soda

¼ tsp. baking powder

1 tsp. salt

1⅓ cups water

½ cup crushed peppermint candy

Instructions:

Grease and flour two 9-inch round cake pans. Preheat the oven to 350°F. Combine the butter, sugar, eggs, and vanilla and beat on high speed for 3 minutes. Combine the flour, cocoa, baking soda, baking powder, and salt in a separate bowl. Add the flour mixture alternately with the water to the butter mixture. Stir only until combined. Add the candy. Pour into the cake pans. Bake for 30–35 minutes. Cool before removing from pan. Decorate with creamy white icing and candy canes.

For little children everywhere

A joyous season still we make,

We bring our precious gifts to them,

Even for the dear Child Jesus' sake.

Phoebe Cary

HOLIDAY TIPS FOR DOGS

❅ When guests come to your house during the holidays, do not sniff them or jump on them.

❅ The Christmas tree is off limits! That means: don't tinkle on it, don't try to eat it, and don't try to knock it over.

❅ Christmas presents are not to be unwrapped unless they have your name on them.

❅ Don't eat off the buffet table when no one is looking; it is okay to beg.

❅ If your master puts you outside, it is perfectly understandable if you howl.

HOLIDAY TIPS FOR CATS

❄ Do not rub against any guest that visits—this is especially important to remember if a guest is wearing pantyhose.

❄ Presents wrapped in colorful metallic paper will be a temptation, but you must resist temptation!

❄ Under no circumstances should you extend your claws when guests are trying to pet you.

❄ Do not jump on the counters when they are set up as a buffet line.

❄ If you need to, it is okay to hide under the bed until the party is over.

It is good to be
children sometimes,
and never better than at *Christmas,*
when its mighty
Founder was a child himself.

Charles Dickens

Were I a philosopher, I should write a philosophy of toys, showing that nothing else in life need be taken seriously, and that Christmas Day in the company of children is one of the few occasions on which men become entirely alive.

Robert Lynd

Christmas
CORNER

Fascinating Facts and Trivia

Let's dance and sing and make good cheer,

For Christmas comes but once a year.

George Alexander Macfarren

British dogs have it made. Seven out of ten are said to receive Christmas gifts from their owners.

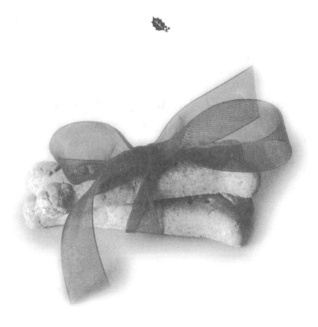

The infamous **Henry VIII** took it upon himself to serve turkey at his Christmas table. Until he made this gutsy departure from tradition, the goose had been the Christmas fowl of choice.

The oft-disparaged **mince pie** is thought to have originated as an offering of sweetmeats presented to the Vatican on Christmas Eve. Some were actually fashioned into the shape of a manger.

The term *Yuletide* originated when Anglo-Saxon families carved a Yule log each Christmas from a heavy, oak block and placed it on the floor of their hearth. Each night, it glowed beneath the household fires. By the next holiday season, it was reduced to ash and the family worked to create a re-placement. The installation of the new log was a favorite pre-Christmas ceremony.

Calvin Coolidge was the first to light the outdoor Christmas tree at the White House in a formal ceremony in 1923. The tradition endures to this day.

The General Grant tree, named after Ulysses S. Grant, is one of the tallest giant sequoias in King's Canyon Park. It became America's **national Christmas tree** in 1926.

Animal crackers originated in England and were imported to the United States in the late 1800s. They are uniquely packaged to resemble a circus cage filled with animals. The string handle was created to allow the box to be hung on a Christmas tree.

Christmas trees are as American as apple pie. They are grown in all fifty states, including Alaska and Hawaii.

Today **mistletoe** is associated with sneaking a kiss, but in ancient times it was a symbol of peace and joy originated by the Druids. When enemies came together in the forest to discuss the possibility of peace, they would put down their arms and stand under the mistletoe, establishing a truce until the next day.

The Puritans forbade the singing of **Christmas carols.**

On Christmas Eve, 1926, the world's first singing commercial aired on the radio. Four male singers sang the jingle for **Wheaties Cereal.** The group included an undertaker, a bailiff, a printer, and a businessman. For the next six years, the men were paid $6.00 per singer per week for their musical advertisement.

Robert Louis Stevenson, author of *Treasure Island*, was a thoughtful gent. A friend had complained to him that she greatly disliked the fact that her birthday fell on Christmas Day. When he died, **he left her his birthday** (November 13) in his will.

How many **white Christmases** have there been in England? Just seven in the entire twentieth century. Some think even that small number is a bit embellished. It is said that in England, a white Christmas is defined as one snowflake on the roof of the weather center.

❧

The **twelve days of Christmas** refer to the days between December 24 and January 5.

❧

Charles Dickens took his time before deciding to call his character **Tiny Tim** in *A Christmas Carol*. He considered three other names: Little Larry, Puny Pete, and Small Sam.

❧

UNICEF produced the **first charity Christmas card** in 1949. It was painted by seven-year-old Jitka Samkova of Rudolfo, Czechoslovakia, in appreciation for UNICEF's emergency assistance of food and medicine given to her village. According to Jitka, the painting of children dancing around a maypole depicted "joy going 'round and 'round." It won first prize in UNICEF's competition and therefore became its first Christmas card.

The postmaster of Washington, D.C., in 1822 was appalled when he had to add **sixteen mailmen** during the holiday season just to deal with Christmas cards. He complained to the authorities that the number of cards a person could send should be limited by law. "I don't know what we'll do if this keeps on," he wrote.

Hallmark, founded by brothers Joyce and Rollie Hall, began producing **Christmas cards** in 1915.

There is a debate over which country printed the **first Christmas stamp.** The Canadian map stamp was printed in 1898. In 1937, Austria issued two stamps to commemorate Christmas.

The first **Salvation Army collection kettle** was a large crab pot. Intended to raise cash to pay for a charity Christmas dinner in 1891, it was placed on a San Francisco street—and the rest is history!

There are **two Christmas Islands.** Kiritimati (meaning "Christmas") Island is an island encircled by a lagoon in the Pacific Ocean. Christmas Island is in the Indian Ocean and was named for the day of its discovery in 1643.

The first **Toys for Tots** Christmas toy drive for needy children took place in 1947.

Charles Pajeau invented Tinkertoy® construction sets and introduced them at a toy fair in 1914. When little interest was generated, he hired several midgets, dressed in elf costumes, to play with the toys in a display window at a Chicago department store during the Christmas season. A year later, over a million sets of **Tinkertoys** had been sold.

The French refer to Christmas as **Noël**, which is derived from the phrase "*les bonnes nouvelles.*" The phrase literally means "the good news" and refers to the Gospel.

In 1914, an unsanctioned truce materialized between the Germans and the British, who were fighting along the western front during Christmastime. The soldiers were within yards of one another in their respective foxholes. On Christmas Eve they decided to lay down their arms and actually visited in the no-man's-land between their trenches. They exchanged gifts such as cake and cigars and even sang songs, including the beloved carol **"Silent Night."** Although the respite was short-lived, it gave new meaning to the word *truce.*

Everyone knows that Jesus was born in a **stable,** but only the very well-informed know that the stable was actually a cave. Caves were routinely used as stables during Bible times. They provided a more temperature-regulated place for the animals during the cold of winter and intense heat of summer.

The **poinsettia,** a flowering plant from Mexico, is also known as Christmas Star. It was introduced to the United States in 1825.

George Washington and his men had a couple of pretty bad Christmas nights. In 1776, they crossed the Delaware River under terrible conditions. If they thought Christmas night of 1777 would be better, they were mistaken. They were camped at Valley Forge that year and ate a pitiful Christmas dinner of fowl cooked in a broth of turnips, cabbage, and potatoes.

British soldiers actively serving on Christmas Day get a special treat—their commanding officers serve them dinner.

Christmas **fruitcake** is the gift that keeps on giving. Over the long term, it simply becomes tastier and tastier. In olden times, it was soaked in liquor to keep down the mold, then coated with powdered sugar. Stored in a tightly closed container, some have been known to last for as long as twenty-five years.

President Harry Truman said a prayer before lighting the **national Christmas tree** during the holiday season in 1951. He probably had no idea what he was starting. Three years later, the National Christmas Tree Ceremony became the "Christmas Pageant of Peace," complete with a life-sized nativity scene and eight reindeer from Alaska.

Theodore Roosevelt was a man of principle, and as a staunch conservationist, he thought it improper to cut trees and display them indoors. He banned the practice in his home even while living in the White House. His children, however, ignored his edict and smuggled them into their bedrooms.

The first states in the United States to declare Christmas a **legal holiday** were Alabama, Louisiana, and Arkansas: Alabama in 1836, and Louisiana and Arkansas in 1838.

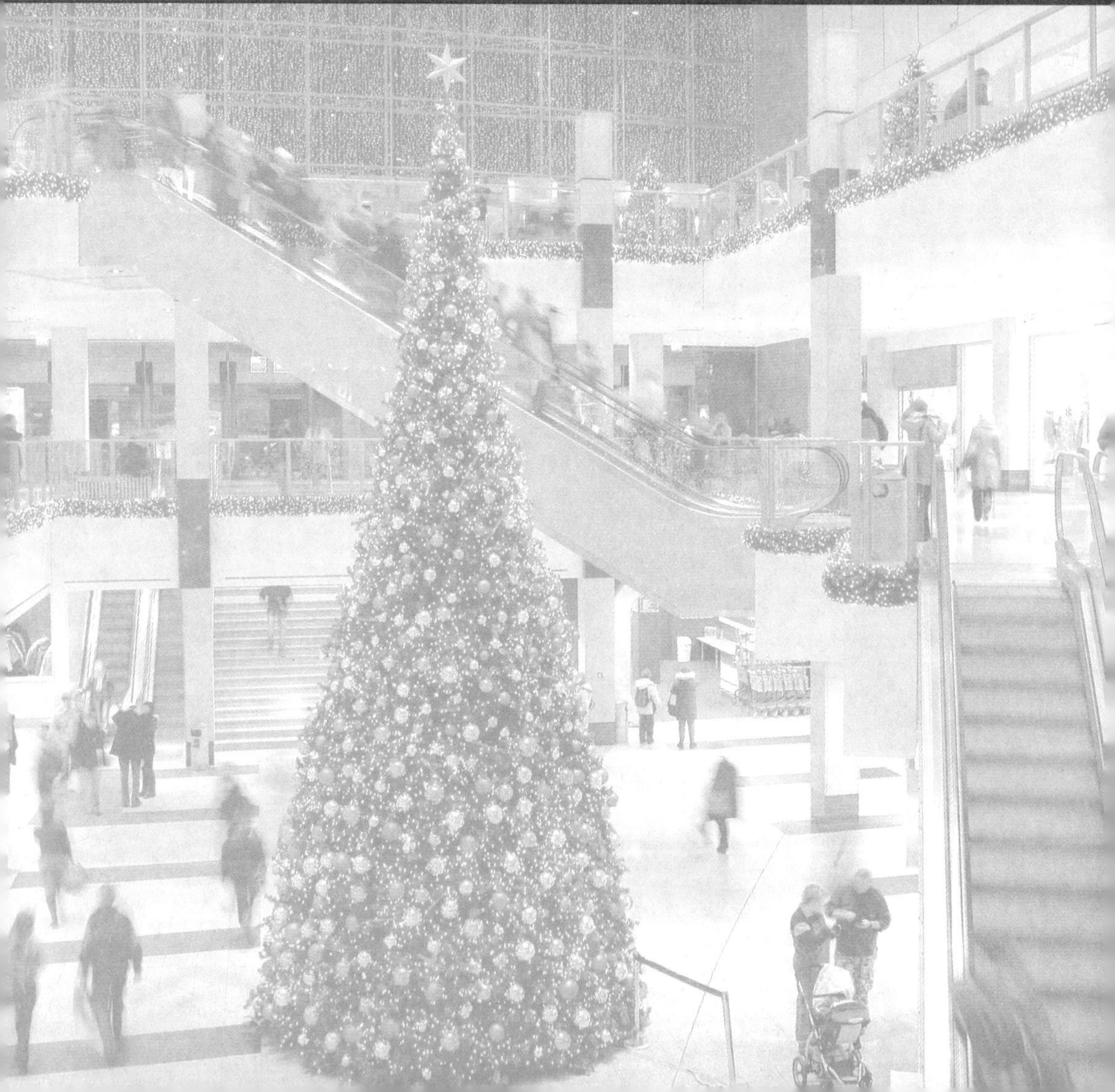

In the 1500s in Europe, it became popular to shorten the Greek word for Christ—*Xristos*—to X. This is where the shortened form **Xmas** originated. Advertisers loved it. It took up less space and has the same number of letters as the word *sale*.

The Christmas holidays are the most popular time of the year to buy **diamonds.**

A **Christmas club savings account,** which allowed a person to make regular deposits of a fixed amount of money to be used at Christmas for shopping, began around 1905.

Retailers in this country can earn up to **40 percent** of their annual revenues during the Christmas holiday.

The Message
of the
MANGER

Glory to God in the heavenly heights,

Peace to all men and women on earth who please him.

LUKE 2:14

THE MESSAGE OF THE MANGER

The events surrounding the birth of Jesus Christ happened more than two thousand years ago. We cherish them as religious tradition and cling to the universal truths they portray, but are they really relevant to our lives here in the twenty-first century?

Indeed, they are!

Men and women still long to be restored to re-lationship with God their Creator. The door that opened on that chilly morning in Bethlehem is still wide open today, providing through Jesus Christ a way to the Father. Wrapped inside that indescribable gift is the love, joy, and peace we all crave.

The Christ Child no longer lies in a tiny manger bed, but His Holy Spirit does take up residence in our hearts and lives, changing us forever.

Joy to the world, the Lord is come!

RULER OF THE STARS

Saint Augustine of Hippo

Maker of the sun,
He is made under the sun.
In the Father he remains,
From his mother he goes forth.
Creator of heaven and earth,
He was born on earth under heaven.
Unspeakably wise,
He is wisely speechless.
Filling the world,
He lies in a manger.
Ruler of the stars,
He nurses at his mother's breast.
He is both great in the nature of God,
And small in the form of a servant.

Christmas Eve was a night of song

that wrapped itself about you like a shawl.

But it warmed more than your body.

It *warmed your heart*—filled it, too,

with a melody that would last forever.

Bess Streeter Aldrich

CELEBRATE THE INCARNATION

Can you imagine it? The Holy Trinity sitting down together, discussing the plan to save mankind. How would They redeem Their fallen creation? A blood sacrifice was needed—that much was clear. But there was a sticky point. The sacrifice had to be flawless, and it had to be made by a human being. In the mind of the Trinity, there was absolute agreement. God the Son would go. He would be implanted by the Holy Spirit into the womb of a lowly young virgin. In so doing, God would take on flesh and blood. He would be God Incarnate. From His mother, He would receive His humanity; from God, His Father, perfection and holiness. He would then be a worthy sacrifice for the sin of mankind. A tiny babe would usher in a New Covenant of forgiveness, reconciliation, and eternal peace.

As you read His story, read with an enlightened heart. What a remarkable plan! And what an amazing love God has for us!

LUKE 1–2, THE MESSAGE

So many others have tried their hand at putting together a story of the wonderful harvest of Scripture and history that took place among us, using reports handed down by the original eyewitnesses who served this Word with their very lives. Since I have investigated all the reports in close detail, starting from the story's beginning, I decided to write it all out for you, most honorable Theophilus, so you can know beyond the shadow of a doubt the reliability of what you were taught.

A CHILDLESS COUPLE CONCEIVES

During the rule of Herod, King of Judea, there was a priest assigned service in the regiment of Abijah. His name was Zachariah. His wife was descended from the daughters of Aaron. Her name was Elizabeth. Together they lived honorably before God, careful in keeping to the ways of the commandments and enjoying a clear conscience before God. But they were childless because Elizabeth could never conceive, and now they were quite old.

It so happened that as Zachariah was carrying out his priestly duties before God, working the shift assigned to his regiment, it came his one turn in life to enter the sanctuary of God and burn incense. The congregation was gathered and praying outside the Temple at the hour of the incense offering. Unannounced, an angel of God appeared just to the right of the altar of incense. Zachariah was paralyzed in fear.

But the angel reassured him, "Don't fear, Zachariah. Your prayer has been heard. Elizabeth, your wife, will bear a son by you. You are to name him John. You're going to leap like a gazelle for joy, and not only you—many will delight in his birth. He'll achieve great stature with God.

"He'll drink neither wine nor beer. He'll be filled with the Holy Spirit from the moment he leaves his mother's womb. He will turn many sons and daughters of Israel back to their God. He will herald God's arrival in the style and strength of Elijah, soften the hearts of parents to children, and kindle devout understanding among hardened skeptics—he'll get the people ready for God."

Zachariah said to the angel, "Do you expect me to believe this? I'm an old man and my wife is an old woman." But the angel said, "I am Gabriel, the sentinel of God, sent especially to bring you this glad news. But because you won't believe me, you'll be unable to say a word until the day of your son's birth. Every word I've spoken to you will come true on time—God's time."

Meanwhile, the congregation waiting for Zachariah was getting restless, wondering what was keeping him so long in the sanctuary. When he came out and couldn't speak, they knew he had seen a vision. He continued speechless and had to use sign language with the people.

When the course of his priestly assignment was completed, he went back home. It wasn't long before his wife, Elizabeth, conceived. She went off by herself for five months, relishing her pregnancy. "So, this is how God acts to remedy my unfortunate condition!" she said.

A VIRGIN CONCEIVES

In the sixth month of Elizabeth's pregnancy, God sent the angel Gabriel to the Galilean village of Nazareth to a virgin engaged to be married to a man descended from David. His name was Joseph, and the virgin's name, Mary. Upon entering, Gabriel greeted her:

> *"Good morning!*
> *You're beautiful with God's beauty,*
> *Beautiful inside and out!*
> *God be with you."*

She was thoroughly shaken, wondering what was behind a greeting like that. But the angel assured her, "Mary, you have nothing to fear. God has a surprise for you: You will become pregnant and give birth to a son and call his name Jesus.

> *He will be great,*
> *   be called 'Son of the Highest.'*
> *The Lord God will give him*

the throne of his father David;
He will rule Jacob's house forever—
  no end, ever, to his kingdom."

Mary said to the angel, "But how? I've never slept with a man."
The angel answered,

"The Holy Spirit will come upon you,
  the power of the Highest hover over you;
Therefore, the child you bring to birth
  will be called Holy, Son of God.

"And did you know that your cousin Elizabeth conceived a son, old as she is? Everyone called her barren, and here she is six months pregnant! Nothing, you see, is impossible with God."

And Mary said,

"Yes, I see it all now:
  I'm the Lord's maid, ready to serve.
Let it be with me
  just as you say."

Then the angel left her.

BLESSED AMONG WOMEN

Mary didn't waste a minute. She got up and traveled to a town in Judah in the hill country, straight to Zachariah's house, and greeted Elizabeth. When Elizabeth heard Mary's greeting, the baby in her womb leaped. She was filled with the Holy Spirit, and sang out exuberantly.

> "You're so blessed among women,
>   and the babe in your womb, also blessed!
> And why am I so blessed that
>   the mother of my Lord visits me?
> The moment the sound of your
>   greeting entered my ears,
> The babe in my womb
>   skipped like a lamb for sheer joy.
> Blessed woman, who believed what God said,
>   believed every word would come true!"

And Mary said,

> "I'm bursting with God-news;
>   I'm dancing the song of my Savior God.
> God took one good look at me, and look what happened—
>   I'm the most fortunate woman on earth!

What God has done for me will never be forgotten,
  the God whose very name is holy, set apart from all others,
His mercy flows in wave after wave
  on those who are in awe before him.
He bared his arm and showed his strength,
  scattered the bluffing braggarts.
He knocked tyrants off their high horses,
  pulled victims out of the mud.
The starving poor sat down to a banquet,
  the callous rich were left out in the cold.
He embraced his chosen child, Israel;
  he remembered and piled on the mercies, piled them high.
It's exactly what he promised,
  beginning with Abraham and right up to now.

Mary stayed with Elizabeth for three months and then went back to her own home.

THE BIRTH OF JOHN

When Elizabeth was full-term in her pregnancy, she bore a son. Her neighbors and relatives, seeing that God had overwhelmed her with mercy, celebrated with her.

On the eighth day, they came to circumcise the child and were calling him Zachariah after his father. But his mother intervened: "No. He is to be called John."

"But," they said, "no one in your family is named that." They used sign language to ask Zachariah what he wanted him named.

Asking for a tablet, Zachariah wrote, "His name is to be John." That took everyone by surprise. Surprise followed surprise—Zachariah's mouth was now open, his tongue loose, and he was talking, praising God!

A deep, reverential fear settled over the neighborhood, and in all that Judean hill country people talked about nothing else. Everyone who heard about it took it to heart, wondering, "What will become of this child? Clearly, God has his hand in this."

Then Zachariah was filled with the Holy Spirit and prophesied,

> "Blessed be the Lord, the God of Israel;
>   he came and set his people free.
> He set the power of salvation in the center of our lives,
>   and in the very house of David his servant,
> Just as he promised long ago
>   through the preaching of his holy prophets:

Deliverance from our enemies
  and every hateful hand;
Mercy to our fathers,
  as he remembers to do what he said he'd do,
What he swore to our father Abraham—
  a clean rescue from the enemy camp,
So we can worship him without a care in the world,
  made holy before him as long as we live.

"And you, my child, 'Prophet of the Highest,'
  will go ahead of the Master to prepare his ways,
Present the offer of salvation to his people,
  the forgiveness of their sins.
Through the heartfelt mercies of our God,
  God's Sunrise will break in upon us,
Shining on those in the darkness,
  those sitting in the shadow of death,
Then showing us the way, one foot at a time,
  down the path of peace."

The child grew up, healthy and spirited. He lived out in the desert until the day he made his prophetic debut in Israel.

THE BIRTH OF JESUS

About that time Caesar Augustus ordered a census to be taken throughout the Empire. This was the first census when Quirinus was governor of Syria. Everyone had to travel to his own ancestral home-town to be accounted for. So Joseph went from the Galilean town of Nazareth up to Bethlehem in Judah, David's town, for the census. As a descendant of David, he had to go there. He went with Mary, his fian-cée, who was pregnant.

While they were there, the time came for her to give birth. She gave birth to a son, her firstborn. She wrapped him in a blanket and laid him in a manger, because there was no room in the hostel.

AN EVENT FOR EVERYONE

There were sheepherders camping in the neighborhood. They had set night watches over their sheep. Suddenly, God's angel stood among them and God's glory blazed around them. They were terrified. The angel said, "Don't be afraid. I'm here to announce a great and joyful event that is meant for everybody, worldwide: A Savior has just been born in David's town, a Savior who is Messiah and Master. This is what you're to look for: a baby wrapped in a blanket and lying in a manger."

At once the angel was joined by a huge angelic choir singing God's praises:

> "Glory to God in the heavenly heights,
> Peace to all men and women on earth who please him."

As the angel choir withdrew into heaven, the sheepherders talked it over. "Let's get over to Bethlehem as fast as we can and see for ourselves what God has revealed to us." They left, running, and found Mary and Joseph, and the baby lying in the manger. Seeing was believing. They told everyone they met what the angels had said about this child. All who heard the sheepherders were impressed.

Mary kept all these things to herself, holding them dear, deep within herself. The sheepherders returned and let loose, glorifying and praising God for everything they had heard and seen. It turned out exactly the way they'd been told!

BLESSINGS

When the eighth day arrived, the day of circumcision, the child was named Jesus, the name given by the angel before he was conceived.

Then when the days stipulated by Moses for purification were complete, they took him up to Jerusalem to offer him to God as commanded in God's Law: "Every male who opens the womb shall be a holy offering to God," and also to sacrifice the "pair of doves or two young pigeons" prescribed in God's Law.

In Jerusalem at the time, there was a man, Simeon by name, a good man, a man who lived in the prayerful expectancy of help for Israel. And the Holy Spirit was on him. The Holy Spirit had shown him that he would see the Messiah of God before he died. Led by the Spirit, he entered the Temple. As the parents of the child Jesus brought him in to carry out the rituals of the Law, Simeon took him into his arms and blessed God:

"God, you can now release your servant;
   release me in peace as you promised.
With my own eyes I've seen your salvation;
   it's now out in the open for everyone to see:
A God-revealing light to the non-Jewish nations,
   and of glory for your people Israel."

Jesus' father and mother were speechless with surprise at these words. Simeon went on to bless them, and said to Mary his mother,

"This child marks both the failure and
   the recovery of many in Israel,
A figure misunderstood and contradicted—

> *the pain of a sword-thrust through you—*
> *But the rejection will force honesty,*
>   *as God reveals who they really are."*

Anna the prophetess was also there, a daughter of Phanuel from the tribe of Asher. She was by now a very old woman. She had been married seven years and a widow for eighty-four. She never left the Temple area, worshiping night and day with her fastings and prayers. At the very time Simeon was praying, she showed up, broke into an anthem of praise to God, and talked about the child to all who were waiting expectantly for the freeing of Jerusalem.

When they finished everything required by God in the Law, they returned to Galilee and their own town, Nazareth. There the child grew strong in body and wise in spirit. And the grace of God was on him.

A greater story,

    a truer story,

        has never been told.

CELEBRATE HIM THIS

SEASON

Attribution Index

Harrington, Cassandra M.
Writer of Inspriational Quotations

Harris, Lydia E.
Contributing Story Writer

Havergal, Frances Ridley (1836–1879)
English Poet and Hymnist

Havner, Vance (1901–1986)
Church Pastor and Author/Speaker

Henry, O. (1862–1910)
Pen name for William Sydney Porter
American Master of Short-story Writing

Hershey, Lenore
Magazine Editor

Heston, Charlton (1924–2008)
Film Actor

Hillis, Burton
Author

Holmes, Marjorie
Christian Fiction Author

Hope, Bob (1903–2003)
Academy Award-winning Entertainer

Hopkins Jr., John H. (1820–1891)
Theologian and Hymnist

Irving, Washington (1783–1859)
American Essayist, Historian, and Author

Jacobsen,Sonja
Contributing Writer

Jaynes, Sharon
Contributing Writer

Jones, W. C.
Author

Keller, Helen (1880–1968)
American Author, Activist, and Lecturer

Knight, John A.
Minister and Church Administrator

Kopp, Nancy Julien
Contributing Story Writer

Laubach, Frank C. (1884–1970)
Christian Evangelical Missionary

Lebar, Lois (1907–1998)
Christian Educator and Author

Longfellow, Henry Wadsworth (1807–1882)
American Poet, Educator, and Linguist

Luther, Martin (1483–1546)
German Monk, Theologian, University Professor,
and Church Reformer

Lynd, Robert (1892–1970)
American Sociologist and Author

Mabie, Hamilton Wright (1846–1916)
American Essayist, Editor, Critic, and Lecturer

Macfarren, George Alexander (1813–1887)
English Composer

MacLaren, Alexander (1826–1910)
Preacher and Expositor

McKibben, Frank
Writer of Inspirational Quotations

Medley, Paul
Writer of Inspirational Quotations

Mitchell, Janet Lynn
Contributing Story Writer

Mohr, Josef (1792–1848)
Austrian Priest and Composer

Norton, Marie
Contributing Story Writer

Pahro, Agnes M.
Writer of Inspirational Quotations

Patri, Angelo (1876–1965)
Italian American Author and Educator

Pickthall, Marjorie Lowry Christie (1883–1922)
Poet and Short-story Writer

Rice, Helen Steiner (1900–1981)
American Poet, Author, and Writer/Editor of
Greeting Cards

Rice, John Richard (1895–1980)
Evangelist, Pastor, Editor of Christian Newspaper

Richardson, Randy
Contributing Writer

Rogers, Dale Evans (1912–2001)
American Leading Lady of Musical Westerns

Rossetti, Christina (1830–1894)
English Poet

Saint Augustine of Hippo (354–430)
Bishop, Philosopher, and Theologian

Saint John of the Cross (1542–1591)
Reformer, Carmelite friar, and Priest

Schulz, Charles (1922–2000)
American Cartoonist (*Peanuts* Comic Strip)

Sears, Edmund Hamilton (1810–1876)
Parish Minister, Theologian, and Author

Seigle, D.V.
Contributing Writer

Sockman, Ralph Washington (1889–1970)
Writer

Spencer, William Robert (1769–1834)
English Poet and Humorist

Stevenson, Robert Louis (1850–1894)
Scottish Novelist, Poet, and Travel Writer

Tennyson, Alfred Lord (1809–1892)
English Poet

Thatcher, Margaret
Former Prime Minister of the United Kingdom

Thurman, Howard (1899–1981)
American Author, Philosopher, Theologian, Educator, and Civil Rights Leader

Truman, Trudy
Contributing Writer

Turner, Nancy Byrd (1880–1971)
American Author and Poet

Valentine, D.
Contributing Writer

Van Dyke, Henry
American Author, Educator, and Clergyman

Wagner, Wilhelm Richard (1813–1883)
German Composer, Conductor, and Essayist

Wallace, Lew (1827–1905)
Lawyer, Governor, Union General, Statesman,
and Author

Watts, Isaac (1674–1748)
Preacher, Poet, and Popular English Hymnist

Wesley, Charles (1707–1788)
Minister and Prolific Hymnist

Whipp, Deborah
American Poet

Whittier, John Greenleaf (1807–1892)
American Quaker Poet

Winkworth, Catherine (1827–1878)
Translator of German Hymns and Carols

Yale, Elsie Duncan (1873–1956)
Songwriter, Composer, and Dramatist

Young, John Freeman (1820–1885)
Protestant Minister, Editor, and Translator

References

Unless otherwise indicated, all Scripture quotations are taken from *The Message*, copyright © by Eugene H. Peterson 1993, 1994, 1995, 1996, 2000, 2001, 2002. Used by permission of NavPress Publishing Group.

Scripture quotations marked NLT are taken from the *Holy Bible, New Living Translation,* copyright © 1996. Used by permission of Tyndale House Publishers, Inc., Wheaton, Illinois 60189. All rights reserved.

Scripture quotations marked NIV are taken from the *Holy Bible: New International Version*® NIV®. Copyright 1973, 1978, 1984 by International Bible Society. Used by permission of Zondervan. All rights reserved.

Scripture quotations marked NKJV are taken from the *New King James Version*®. Copyright © 1982 by Thomas Nelson, Inc. Used by permission. All rights reserved.

Scripture quotations marked NCV are taken from the *New Century Version*®. Copyright © 2005 by Thomas Nelson, Inc. Used by permission. All rights reserved.

Scripture quotations marked NRSV are taken from *The New Revised Standard Version Bible.* Copyright © 1989 by the Division of Christian Education of the National Council of the Churches of Christ in the United States of America and are used by permission. All rights reserved.

Scripture quotations marked KJV are taken from the *King James Version* of the Bible.

Notes

1. "A Christmas Kind of Love." Story written by Janet Lynn Mitchell. Used by permission of the author.

2. "Love, I Corinthians 13—Style." Poem taken from *Celebrating a Christ-Centered Christmas: Ideas from A to Z* by Sharon Jaynes (Chicago, IL: Moody Publishers, 2001), p. 53. Used by permission of the author. All rights reserved.

3. "Francis's Oyster Dressing." Recipe written by Rebecca Currington. Used by permission of the author.

4. "Away in a Manger." Story written by Kathe Campbell. Used by permission of the author.

5. "A Christmas for Julie." Story written by Nancy Julien Kopp. Used by permission of the author.

6. "The Ten Commandments of Christmas." Poem written by Paul Ciniraj. Used by permission of the author.

7. "A Refugee Camp Christmas." Story written by Renie Burghardt. Used by permission of the author.

8. "The Robe Less Traveled." Story written by Todd and Jedd Hafer. Used by permission of the authors.

9. "A Christmas Letter to My Mom." Story written by Kathleen Anderson. Used by permission of the author.

10. "Benard's Story." Story written by Deena C. Bouknight. Used by permission of the author.

11. "Welcome Christmas." Poem written by Sonja Jacobsen. Used by permission of Snapdragon Group℠ Editorial Services.

12. "A Night Wrapped in Song." Story written by Lydia E. Harris. Used by permission of the author.

13. "The Best Christmas Present Ever." Story written by Nancy Julien Kopp. Used by permission of the author.

14. "The Spirit of Christmas." Poem written by Randy Richardson. Used by permission of the author.

15. "The Snow Globe." Story written by Marie Norton. Used by permission of the author.

Wake Technical Community College
WITHDRAWN
Raleigh, NC 27603-5696

DATE DUE

JAN 0 3 2011

WITHDRAWN

FEB – '09